Ignite Your Leadership

Proven Tools for Leaders to Energize Teams, Fuel
Momentum, and Accelerate Results

Second Edition

Kathy Sparrow, Neel Raman,
and Nine Other International Thought Leaders

AUTHORS PLACE
— P R E S S —

Published by Authors Place Press

9885 Wyecliff Drive, Suite 200

Highlands Ranch, CO 80126

Authorsplace.com

Manufactured in the United States of America.

ISBN: 978-1-62865-775-3

To our mentor and friend, Jack Canfield

Praise for *Ignite Your Leadership*

"Why read *Ignite Your Leadership*? Because in this book, wise woman Kathy Sparrow and her co-authors offer clear perspectives and pathways to demonstrate healthier, more effective leadership—the kind of leadership that empowers you and others to bring wisdom to the challenges we face, as individuals, organizations and communities, and societies—and the kind of leadership that cultivates the conditions where everyone has the opportunity to thrive."

~ Renee Moorefield, PhD, CEO of Wisdom Works, leader in the global conscious leadership movement and creator of the Be Well Lead Well Pulse® assessment

"*Ignite Your Leadership* is as relevant as ever. Our pace of life is fast, mainly due to technological developments. When changes occur that affect company processes, this requires the cooperation of employees within teams. Businesses need world-class leadership to withstand challenging conditions. Above all, managers need to ignite the inner flame in themselves and others. That is why I appreciate the structure of Ignite Your Leadership, which starts with a leader and ends with the whole company."

The current situation around the global pandemic has shown precisely that leadership is essential not only in the business environment but in science, healthcare, culture, politics, or public administration, as well.

~ Tomáš Hájek, Executive Director, ADMEZ (Association of Direct Marketing, E-Commerce and Mail Order Business), Prague, Czech Republic

"*Ignite Your Leadership* is a must-read book to take your personal leadership, team leadership, and organizational leadership to a much higher level. What Jack Canfield did in *Chicken Soup for the Soul* to inspire and engage, Neel Raman and his co-authors do for emerging leaders in *Ignite Your Leadership*. The components of leadership are explained in simple, easy-to-understand terms, and the book provides practical examples you can easily apply, in real-time."

~ Teresa de Grosbois, #1 International bestselling author of *Mass Influence* and founder of the Evolutionary Business Council

"This book is an inspiring and practical read for effective leaders at all levels of business who are committed to their own continued growth as well as to the care and growth of those they lead. *Ignite Your Leadership* authors present rich stories and tools on key topics which will inspire you to purposeful action. As a leader, it is important to get to the essence of what is needed at this time by you and by the leaders in your organization. You will come away from reading this book being affirmed to continue your growth, as well as holding new models and tools to create success in your personal and professional life. These authors, seasoned practitioners from around the globe, candidly share their insights for you and your organization's well-being."

~ Anita Sanchez, PhD, author of *The Four Sacred Gifts: Indigenous Wisdom for Modern Times,* member of the Transformational Leadership Council

"This is a diverse, but satisfyingly coherent set of useful ideas, concepts, tools, and tips from a range of experienced professionals who are clearly passionate about and highly skilled at what they do.

A book generous in its stories, anecdotes, and practical examples by enthusiastic authors wanting to be of help and service to leaders everywhere, *Ignite* is a testament to what can be achieved when committed people join together to do something worthwhile."

~ Andrew Simon, MEd, BEd, Founding Director and CEO YE Performance Architects, Canberra, Australia, member of the Board of the International Leadership Association

"As the Chief Heartrepreneur™ at www.heartrepreneur, I believe leaders must shift to inspiring people and to caring about people with their heart. *Ignite Your Leadership* is a practical read for leaders who want to be more effective and grow their organizations."

~Terri Levine, International bestselling author of *Turbocharge How to Transform Your Business as a Heartrepreneur™*

"Having studied leadership for decades and having read literally hundreds of books on leadership over the years, I can tell you with certainty that *Ignite Your Leadership* stands out as a must-read. The old, traditional ways of leading organizations—through top-down authority and one-upmanship—no longer work. These diverse authors are 100% correct in their vision of how we must lead in the twenty-first century, which is through authenticity, transparency, connection, positivity, and inclusion. They embrace the fact that true leadership begins within. They teach us that leaders are learners, constantly improving themselves in order to do, and be, their best. They share true stories that illuminate the Success Principles they espouse. These authors and I share a mentor, Jack Canfield, who wrote *The Success Principles*. Jack's spirit of uplifting integrity permeates this book."

~ Cheryl Bonini Ellis, speaker, executive trainer, high-performance coach, and author of *Becoming Deliberate: Changing the Game of Leadership from the Inside Out*

"If you are a leader—read this! *Ignite Your Leadership* offers leading edge tools and guidance on how leaders can better inspire and serve their people to coax the best from their teams. I always say, 'Life's a classroom, not a test.' I've observed so many of my clients struggle as they seek to understand how they fit into their jobs, often frozen in place from conflicting company dynamics; many of them are stressed, fearful of failure, and not contributing well. As a committed leader in the field of human development, I've observed the most successful among us have clarity about what's most important in both work and life. This book helps leaders learn to banish fear among their employees and help their people lean-in to discovering how to function better with clarity, confidence, and greater trust when bringing their authentic best to work each day. Lynden Kidd and her co-authors bring wise, thoughtful, and fresh voices to the conversation about leadership as a lynchpin in human development, sharing stories and ideas that transform leadership and make companies stronger as a result."

~ Kimberly Giles, The "LIFEadvice" Expert, master executive life coach, author of *Choosing Clarity* and Professional Speaker, founder and president of Claritypoint International

"Alive with insights, concepts, and new ways of thinking about leadership, *Ignite Your Leadership* is for leaders who are genuine about leading authentically. It starts where all great leaders start—

with themselves. Original and penetrating, this is an excellent book."

~ Scarlet Bennett, author of *Striking Out*

"Leadership at the heart level goes beyond the techniques and the tools for leaders. It requires them to engage with full their personality not just to play another role while doing their job. It is real, it is right, and it is worthwhile!"

~ Mojmír Boucník CFO, Economia (leading Czech publisher)

"Whether you are running a business with thousands of employees, leading a team of ten, facilitating a business mastermind, or participating in a family meeting, being a productive, thoughtful leader remains an invaluable skill. Read any chapter in *Ignite Your Leadership: Proven Tools for Leaders to Energize Teams, Fuel Momentum, and Accelerate Results,* and let it serve as a catalyst for insights and breakthroughs that you can apply to expanding the richness of your business and personal life."

~ George C. Huang, M.D., cash flow acceleration strategist and co-author, *Create the Business Breakthrough You Want*

"Leadership is about people. About inspiring them, serving them, caring for them, and caring about them. The leader who understands the hierarchy of people's needs and responses will succeed. Leadership is also about emotion. It is about reaching people on an emotional level."

~ Michaela Pfeiferova, international real estate director

Table of Contents

Foreword

by Jack Canfield

I believe there has never been a time in the world where conscious transformational leaders have been more needed—in government, education, health care, corporations, small businesses, and philanthropic organizations. What is clear is that the problems in the world cannot be solved by old ways of thinking or old methods of leadership. A new way of looking at things and a new way of presenting solutions that come from a much higher place of awareness is required.

To help meet this need, I created the Transformational Leadership Council and developed my Train the Trainer program. I am now thrilled by the fact that a number of my Train the Trainer graduates, led by Kathy Sparrow and Neel Raman, have come together to create this valuable resource—*Ignite Your Leadership: Proven Tools for Leaders to Energize Teams, Fuel Momentum, and Accelerate Results.*

A basic premise of transformational leadership is that leadership needs to happen from the inside out. This means that the leader must transform him- or herself first before they can effectively transform others or their organization. Leaders need to first understand who they are, what their limiting beliefs are, and what their fears are. It is only when they are aware of them and can transcend them that they can bring forward what needs to emerge

1

in that moment so that the true needs of the individuals and the organization can be met.

The contributions in this book cover a wide range of core topics regarding transformational leadership—developing one's own self-awareness, leading from the heart, the power of intention, creating high employee and team engagement, creating a safe space that fosters creativity and innovation, the power of transparency, and much, much more.

Having worked with the principles and techniques presented in *Ignite Your Leadership* for more than forty years, I can promise you that applying what you learn in this book will help you become a better leader. Knowing that the path of leadership is a life-long journey of exploration, application, feedback, and learning, I wish you well on your leadership journey as you transform yourself into a better leader.

Jack Canfield
New York Times Bestselling Author
Founder of the Transformational Leadership Council

Introduction

I t's an honor to be giving birth to this project for a second time. When *Ignite Your Leadership: Proven Tools for Leaders to Energize Teams, Fuel Momentum, and Accelerate Results* was first released in early 2017, we knew leadership skills and development needed attention, and we had no idea the world would be in greater need of leadership guidance now more than ever before. Interestingly, as I reflect upon my coauthors, our leadership, and our professional development, we've all taken risks to be seen and heard in a more expansive way.

In the first rendition of this Introduction, I previously wrote, as a writer, I know that some projects begin knocking at the door long before we *believe* we are ready to take them on. This project was one of those.

I was sitting in the back of one of Jack Canfield's training rooms when a fellow member of the assisting team whispered to me, "We need to do something together—as a group." The idea of a book was bantered about, one that included graduates of Jack's exclusive Train the Trainer program.

Yet, behind my momentary realization that a project like the one you are about to read was not only possible, inwardly I knew it would be fraught with obstacles, hurdles, and challenges—one every leader faces no matter if they're leading a family, a community, an organization, a department, or an international corporation. I tabled the idea. It seemed too large. Despite my experience in the traditional publishing world as a writer and an editor, the little voice inside of me said, "Who am I to do this?"

Four months later, I was Skyping with my friend, Neel Raman, who was also a graduate of my 2011 Train the Trainer class, and he said, "Kathy, why don't you do a book for those of us who passed through Jack's programs?" I groaned. Neel was, by this time, the third person to say this to me in as many months. The Universe was knocking a little harder on my door, and I knew I had to say "yes."

Like all good leaders, I realized I couldn't do this alone. So, I invited Neel to be my partner, my co-leader. Ultimately, I knew that with my background in publishing, spanning three decades on both sides of the editorial desk, I would hold much of the responsibility; however, I needed a good person by my side to help me brainstorm ideas, head the launch, and be there to make some tough decisions. In reflection, I have to chuckle that we unconsciously formed a team that is representative of the global face of leadership, possessing masculine and feminine perspectives about what it takes to be a good leader. And with Neel being an Aussie, and me living in the Unites States, the Northern and Southern Hemispheres are covered as well.

The first step was to create a list of people to invite into the project. I didn't want this to be like one of the other books so often brought about by collaboration—pay a lot of money and have your picture on the cover with some big celebrity coach, and call yourself a best-selling author. I hail from the mainstream publishing world having held positions on staff and as a freelancer. Credibility ranks very high in my book. We needed good contributors and ones who could write. And there had to be some sense to the order of chapters.

Neel and I had several Skype meetings, sent numerous emails back and forth, and then we met at Jack's Breakthrough to Success in 2013, where we were both assisting. We refined our list and then began creating the plan. Approximately one year after the idea was whispered in my ear, we sent out letters of invitation to sixteen authors. A few jumped in right away, and more came on board in December. The plan was to have drafts of the chapters in hand by January 31, 2014, and the book published and launched by May 31, 2014, through my company.

Another thing I know as a writer—and one that I resisted in this project—is that when we say "yes" to a writing project, the Universe then takes over as project manager. I expected my leadership skills were going to be put to the test. I stumbled on many occasions. I didn't have a clear exit plan for those who originally decided to join the project and then opted to leave. And because I am friends with those involved in the project, I was soft on my deadlines. Originally, we had sixteen authors ready to contribute. Many left the project, in part due to the delay in production, and in part—others were not ready to say "yes" to bringing their message into the world in bigger way.

Furthermore, I likely used the delays by others to stall as well. In Steven Pressfield's words, I wasn't ready to "turn pro." I was afraid that by stepping out into the world as a leader with my message of "The Power of Your Story: Discovering Your Why, Dissolving Your Why Nots" my invisibility would dissolve, and I'd be "seen." Life would be complicated. I'd have greater responsibilities. Worse yet, I might be judged by my family for stepping out of my role as mother, daughter, sister—for living *my* story—not merely filling a role in theirs.

Sheryl Sandberg, COO of Facebook, and author of *Lean In: Women, Work, and the Will to Lead* says, "Fear is at the root of so many of the barriers that women face. Fear of not being liked. Fear of making the wrong choice. Fear of drawing negative attention. Fear of overreaching. Fear of being judged. Fear of failure. And the holy trinity of fear: the fear of being a bad mother/wife/daughter."

I believe that men face the fear of not being good enough in the eyes of their loved ones as well. Neel echoed these sentiments in the final phases of this project. It's an affliction that causes many leaders—or leaders-to-be—to hesitate, to procrastinate, or to self-sabotage.

However, this is what I do know about great leaders: They are willing to be vulnerable, authentic, and transparent. And that's what you'll experience in each of the chapters that follow. These authors—my friends and colleagues—are willing to take the risk to admit mistakes, fears, and to provide evidence that success is possible even if we momentarily give in to our fears and "play amateur."

What You're About to Experience

Ignite Your Leadership: Proven Tools for Leaders to Energize Teams, Fuel Momentum, and Accelerate Results is divided into three sections containing a total of eleven chapters.

In Section 1, the authors explore the theme of "Leading Yourself."

The section begins with my own Chapter 1, "The Power of Your Story: Discovering Your Why, Dissolving Your Why Nots." Here, I discuss the theory that many of us continue to play the roles created for us by our parents, teachers, partners, children, and even bosses, because at the root of all of our actions is the desire to be loved and accepted. However, in seeking the approval of others, we're doing a disservice to ourselves and to the world. We're not stepping fully into our leadership, nor are we fulfilling our missions at our workplace, with our families, or in our communities. To break the hold that our past has upon us, we need to discover our "why" and dissolve the "why nots."

In Chapter 2, "Conscious Leadership: Leading Others by First Leading Yourself," Pete Winiarski shares his beliefs that as business leaders strive to transform their company results, they have the challenge of enabling their teams to perform at their best. Achieving peak performance requires leaders to develop a higher awareness of both themselves and others. *Conscious Leaders* start by building a conscious awareness of themselves first, and then build a conscious awareness of others around them, including their teams, their peers, and other people in their sphere of influence. When leaders are *Conscious of Self*, they inspire others by their personal results and style. When leaders are *Conscious of Others*, they build followership and create a team that is capable of great performance and transforming company results. This chapter provides an overview of *Conscious Leadership* and describes the above characteristics.

In Chapter 3, Nathalie Osborn contributes, "Powering Personal Energy: The kW of Energized Leadership." She shares how to plug into your own personal power and fuel your full leadership potential. This chapter reveals three simple "kW"s to enrich your personal and professional life, showing you how to recharge, refuel, and renew your own personal energy, as well as how to ignite this spark within others and your organization. She emphasizes that our personal energy is our most renewable and powerful resource. Our capacity to be effective, productive, successful, and happy leaders is driven by how well we are able to manage, recharge, and refuel our own personal energy.

In Chapter 4, "Your Greatest Leadership Challenge," Neel Raman reminds us we cannot lead others unless we have a high level of self-awareness. He provides a comparison of common leadership expectations, which are often unreliable, with the requirements needed to lead in today's volatile economic, social, and political environment. He offers a plan to overcome our leadership challenges through the LEAD Model—Learn, Enforce, Adjust, and Discover.

In Chapter 5, "Intentional Possibility: The Magic of Happiness and the Power of Change," Sergio Sedas, PhD explores how ordinary people make extraordinary things happen. They start community projects, they organize events, they create hospitals, they design new and exciting products, and they inspire people into greatness. These people that do the extraordinary start with an idea—an idea that inspires them and moves them. With inspired thought, they create possibility by thinking and behaving as if "it" were a reality. They live in this possibility as if it was real.

They have ideas. They commit. They act. Soon, that which started off as an inspired thought takes shape, and that which was born in possibility emerges.

Section 2: "Leading Others" kicks off with **Chapter 6, "Teams that Shine: Creating Conditions for Maximum Engagement."** **Sally Dooley** demonstrates how creating highly engaged teams is an essential goal for every leader. Research consistently shows that the greater the level of engagement, the higher the productivity and the happier the team members will be both inside and outside of work. Yet many leaders feel they don't have the time or the strategy to build a team that shines. This chapter considers five key drivers for engagement: authentic leadership, alignment between roles and strengths, clear linkages between individual and organisational goals, and effective use of two-way feedback. Practical strategies for building these drivers into your leadership practice are also included so leaders can begin to implement these concepts immediately.

In **Chapter 7: "Leadership at the Heart Level: Embracing and Implementing Change to Bring Meaningful Visions to Life,"** **Jaroslav Průša** introduces a fundamentally new approach to leadership. By leveraging strong emotions, and using the five elements of leadership and seven core principles, leaders will be able to harness the innate energy of each situation and facilitate desired changes in people's attitudes and behavior in real time. Moving from unnecessary top-down pressure to inspiring greater trust, engagement, and responsibility, they will improve communication and relationships, and consequently bring their visions to life more easily and with better results.

In Chapter 8: "How to Outfox the Three Subconscious Saboteurs Lurking in Your Workplace," Jane Ransom provides science-proven tools to rescue you and your employees from inner gridlock. That gridlock can appear as various things— disengagement, or lack of willpower, or creative block, etc.—but it's always some form of self-sabotage originating in the subconscious mind. To free you and your employees from three particularly prevalent forms of inner resistance, Ransom offers surprisingly simple yet powerful strategies. Drawing on scientific research, as well as on her experience as a master hypnotist, she shares brain-training strategies you can use right now.

Section Three dives into "Leading Organizations." In Chapter 9, "Leading Change: How to Create True, Meaningful, and Impactful Change in Your Organization," Amina Makhdoom describes how, as a Management Consultant, she has seen all types of business initiatives, from automation, to reducing costs, to innovation projects, and while all of the projects are unique in their own way, and have completely different models to get the return on investment (ROI), they all have one huge, common hurdle: they involve people changing their behavior. Over the years, Amina found that this one hurdle can make or break a project, and it can cause companies to either obtain or lose their ROI. However, she discovered proven strategies that result in internally motivated change within a company—and result in the creation of True Change—one that is motivated from the inside and expressed in the business place, leading to the business results all hope to achieve.

In Chapter 10, "Planning with Passion: Business Strategizing for Inspired Leaders," Connie Whitesell shows you how to take your business planning from a "should do" to an "inspired done!" Through this unique process, you will discover how to create a prosperity plan that moves you forward immediately toward your vision for your work. The "Planning with Passion" system combines the most effective traditional business planning methods with empowering inspirational and accountability techniques to lead you to a step-by-step plan of action that revs you up and takes you to exactly where you want to be—and better.

Finally, in Chapter 11, "Leading a Heart-Centered Pivot and Reset in 3 Steps," Lynden Kidd writes a letter to her young adult daughter, reminding her of the lessons they learned during Lynden's health challenge in 2018. Lynden reflects on how these lessons can be mapped onto any leadership challenge—whether pandemics, racial tensions, or business failures. She shares how personal responsibility, heart-centered decision making, and resilience helped to pivot their lives, not only once but many times.

We're grateful to be able to share this journey with you. To ignite your leadership, turn the page and enjoy the valuable information and wisdom shared by each of these authors.

Kathy Sparrow

Section One
Leading Yourself

CHAPTER 1

The Power of Your Story

Discovering Your Why, Dissolving Your Why Nots

by Kathy Sparrow

My "Why" came to me at a young age. I knew from the time that I spent my summer afternoons reading Marguerite Henry's Chincoteague Pony series and *Seventeen* magazine, that I wanted to be a writer. When I wasn't dreaming of writing and journaling my thoughts, I pretended to be on stage, acting and dancing.

These dreams were far-fetched for the oldest child, female at that, raised in a blue-collar family in a tiny Upstate New York town. My father worked first in a cement plant, running the train, and he later went on to manage the production at an asphalt plant. My mother, while she desired to be a nurse, allowed her familial responsibilities to my siblings, my father, and my grandfather to get in the way. Even though New York City was a mere two-hour drive south along the Taconic Parkway, and many residents in and around my little town were writers, artists, actors, and dancers, I was taught to distrust "those" people and their way of life. It just wasn't how "we" were supposed to live. That point was driven home in earnest by my guidance counselor, Mr. Bowman.

As my mother and I sat in his office, months before I was to enter high school, Mr. Bowman asked, "What do you want to be when you grow up?" Squaring my shoulders, I said, "I want to be a writer, and I'm interested in the theatre."

Mr. Bowman matched my posture, and with his own dramatic flair, he removed the wireframe glasses from his large balding head and placed them on my academic folder. "You'll never be a writer," he said, peering at me with disdain. As the heat rose to my face, I slumped in the hard, oak chair, feeling life being sucked out of me.

Worse yet, my mother never said a word. In the fall, I began my studies in business, learning the art of shorthand, typing, and accounting—skills that were sure to come to my aid if I ever found myself without a husband to care for me.

In the years that followed, I bought into all of the reasons why I couldn't be a writer or an actress. It just wasn't done. People didn't have jobs doing those sorts of things, especially people "like us"— people whose roots were traced to coal mines in Kentucky and eighth grade educations. Their stories were etched deep inside of me, as I sat around kitchen tables, my grandmother's in particular, listening to women's stories of disappointments, illnesses, and dashed hopes for future employment, sprinkled in with the birth of a new grandchild.

While these stories provided me with a greater understanding of what was important to the women in my family, and what sorrows weighed heavily upon their souls, they rarely asked about my hopes and dreams. I was invisible. No one inquired about my life, what I wanted to be when I grew up, or what I feared. I had learned that my place was to be silent. My words were not of importance or of interest to anyone else. Unfortunately, in most instances, the women in my life delivered the message—*Be silent. Don't be seen. Don't rock the boat.*

In my early teens, during a time when I was taking organ lessons, at the prompting of my parents or some other meaningful adult, I shared a new 45—Chicago's *Color My World*—with my organ teacher. My mother stood to the side as I played the song on the record player, crooning and swaying along with the music. I noted the frown on her face and knew later I would pay for her obvious disapproval of my actions.

Mr. Niver smiled, and after the song was over, said that he would try to get the music so that I could learn to play the song. When he left the house, my mother chastised me for wasting his time. The message was clear that what I felt, and what I enjoyed, did not matter. I had also embarrassed her, because my behavior strayed outside the parameters of how a "good" girl conducted herself. The only way I was to be heard in this particular context was playing scales and the devotional hymns that were standard in the music books available to me. From this experience, I learned to keep my dreams and my fears locked within myself, or within my journal—and especially away from her.

I'd like to say that the suppression of my voice ended when I left high school, but by this time the master narrative of the culture in which I was raised was etched into my psyche by father, mother, grandparents, and other adults within the community. My dream of being something different than they were was dashed by their disapproval and their limited expectations of what I was to do with my life. It was a weighty burden to fend off alone without a mentor or role model.

I had one woman—a neighbor whom I called Aunt Veen—who praised me for my intelligence and encouraged me to pursue my dreams. She was a head teller at the local bank by day, but by night, she bowed to her husband and son's demands. Her behavior at home was the conveyor of the dominant message: to be loved and accepted, I'd better follow the rules, particularly those set by the men in my life. Ultimately, I succumbed to the pressure to conform, and the hold of the "why nots" grew stronger.

In my late teens, I worked as a secretary to a lawyer while attending community college, and I married a man with a strong will and an equally strong view of the place of the women in his life. Soon thereafter, I gave birth to two beautiful children. My priorities were predetermined by my husband's traditional views, those he was also raised with. My role as wife and mother came first, and I was to have little or no contact with my friends, particularly those of whom he disapproved. Even the money I earned and the benefits I provided for my family were deemed as insignificant, secondary to his.

Later, my work managing the district office for a United States Congressman was the only place where I had some identity with "power" attached to it. As it was for my Aunt Veen, things were different at home. Multiethnic psychiatrist and author of *Narrative Medicine,* Lewis Mehl-Madrona, MD, PhD, suggests that I was a minor character in other people's stories. Many times, I felt like a vacant face in a movie crowd scene.

My story is a perfect example of how, early in our lives, we follow the rules set down by those who come before us—often without questioning why these rules are in place. However, when we observe our circumstances, we may find that the rules keep the current ruler in power—not for the good of the whole, but for the good of the one or the few.

Many of us commit the error of following the rules of our cultural community, which prevents us from stepping out of our caves and sharing our gifts in the world. Steven Pressfield, acclaimed author of *Turning Pro: Tap Your Inner Power and Create your Life's Work*, says, "Becoming himself [herself] means being different from others and thus, possibly, violating the expectations of the tribe, without whose acceptance and approval, he [she] believes, he [she] cannot survive."

As I entered my twenties, I began questioning the "why nots" of Mr. Bowman. I re-entered college and changed my degree to liberal studies, setting aside the trajectory in business and accounting he prescribed for me in high school. With the encouragement of two of my college professors, I began writing. My talents and gifts rose to the surface, and my portfolio grew. I began editing for magazine and book publishers. Then I began coaching others who also had a dream of writing.

Despite the challenges, mostly beliefs that I accepted from others, I have been a professional writer for nearly thirty years. I am also faculty at the university level in first-year writing programs and in upper-level creative writing courses where I focus primarily on teaching marketing for authors. While I have not formally acted on any stage, I stand in front of the classroom and share my love of writing, encouraging my students to overcome their "why nots." I also lead workshops and deliver keynotes on a number of topics, including "Discovering Our Why and Dissolving Our Why Nots."

Staying Vigilant

Mere awareness of the stories of our youth, however, is not enough to keep those "why nots" at bay. Vigilance is demanded. These stories are deeply embedded in our psyche and attached to those we love most—or whose love and approval we crave. With every new opportunity or new project, the "why not" stories rise to the surface of my awareness. My choice is to either ignore them or to embrace them full on. Many of my stories revolve around the messages of my mother—and my rebuttal of them. Near the end of her life, I had to come to grips with the fact that while she may have loved me, she didn't like me.

I'm different from many members of my family. I've traveled the world and left bad marriages. I'm an adventurer, eagerly searching to discover what's over the next mountain. And probably the most egregious error of all is that I've taken the risk to be seen and to "get above my raising." At one point, a few years ago, my mother said, "You're nothing but a snooty bitch." Initially, I took it

> *We're held hostage by the stories that other people write for us and about us. We don't stop long enough to question why the story was written and whose purpose it serves.*

personally and fell into a heap of tears. We didn't speak for weeks. Then I realized my willingness to step into my greatness made her uncomfortable. She never allowed herself to find her own. She lived under the cloak of her "why nots." The same can be said of my father, who chastised me for "breaking up the family," when I decided to leave my volatile first marriage.

As I shared in the Introduction, Sheryl Sandberg, COO of Facebook and author of *Lean In: Women, Work and the Will to Lead*, says, "Fear is at the root of so many of the barriers that women face. Fear of not being liked. Fear of making the wrong choice. Fear of drawing negative attention. Fear of overreaching. Fear of being judged. Fear of failure, and the holy trinity of fear: the fear of being a bad mother/wife/and daughter."

William Kittredge, author of *Taking Care: Thoughts on Storytelling and Belief*, says:

"We all know a lot of stories and we're in trouble when we don't know which one is ours. Or when the one we inhabit doesn't work anymore, and we stick with it anyway. We have cultural and community stories that contain implicit instructions from a society to its members, telling them what is valuable and how to conduct themselves if they are to preserve the things they cherish."

The same can be said for many of the men I know. They're fearful of being bad fathers, husbands, and sons.

Fear is the enemy of our "Why"—our calling, our passion, our mission. It prevents us from taking our unique place in the world and sharing our gifts so that others may benefit from our courageous acts. It becomes our imprisoner and, in some cases, the executioner. We're held hostage by the stories that other people write for us and about us. We don't stop long enough to question why the story is written and whose purpose it serves. These stories can be of the family, a spouse, a friend, a boss, our culture, and our nation.

When we buy into those limiting and marginalizing stories, our souls are in exile. We spend our days worrying about pleasing others rather than doing what's right for us—and ultimately what's right for our families, our community, and our world.

While society's stability is assured through the adherence of some rules associated with the master narrative and may be important in certain circumstances, the difficulty arises when the master narrative perpetuates falsehoods or dysfunctions. William Kittredge, author of *Taking Care: Thoughts on Storytelling and Belief*, says:

> "We all know a lot of stories, and we're in trouble when we don't know which one is ours. Or when the one we inhabit doesn't work anymore, and we stick with it anyway. We have cultural and community stories that contain implicit instructions from a society to its members, telling them what is valuable and how to conduct themselves if they are to preserve the things they cherish."

In my own family, dysfunction was sustained by my mother's belief that she should "not rock the boat," one that I was expected to uphold. My mother wanted to keep me silent about a number of issues and not only my love of music. Her mantra preserved our relatively peaceful existence in the chaotic environment where alcoholism shadowed our family life. In retrospect, I believe she feared that if I broke my silence and resisted her mandate to stay within the rules of the family and our community, she would be forced to do the same, and the stability of our "normal" family would be shattered. The context would be set for her to search the truth of the rules that governed our lives. She then might be prompted to consider choosing between the life she was expected to live by the rules under which she was raised—one where "you made your bed, now lie in it"—and creating a life of her own making.

When I did rock the boat in my first marriage, several decades after I had internalized my mother's mantra and the mandate of my community, it was partly as the result of my daughter's questioning of her father's tyrannical rule over our household and her plea for me to do the same. While it was difficult at first to accept responsibility to challenge the dysfunction controlling our lives, I was able to do so only after examining how ridiculous most of the rules I was expected to follow really were.

Mehl-Madrona says, "Achieving a pre-narrative awareness is an important tool for deconstruction, for removing our usual assumptions about the world, so we can reflect upon what is essential and what is not, what we prefer and what do we not prefer, and more."

By removing the assumptions—the "why nots"—of those vested in maintaining their power over my life or theirs, I was able to create a new story. Initially, this drove a wedge between my mother and myself, by accentuating our differences rather than our common ground. It was only more than a decade after leaving my first marriage, when she began voicing her opposition to my father's dominance in her life because of his alcohol abuse, that our relationship became closer. While my counter-narrative—the story of my own creation—still caused her some discomfort, she did acknowledged how far I had come in my life, and how hard I've worked to rise above the oppressive forces that have lurked in the shadows throughout much of my life. Her words were a hard-won blessing.

In the 2007 Power of Words Conference, Mehl-Madrona affirmed that our lives can change because individuals have the power to initiate change through the creation of a different story. By challenging the master narrative of my family, school counselor, and other members of the community, I have moved from an invisible member of our family and community to someone who is now seen and heard, not only within the family structure but in the greater community as well. I'm stepping more fully into my "Why." Those tangentially affected by my changes have also been able to take steps in their own lives to create a new story, one of their own making. That is the healing power of story. When we embrace our "Why," we give others permission to do likewise.

Additionally, when we step into the leading role of our own life, rather than continue to play supporting roles in others, we are energized and vitalized. Work is no longer drudgery. It becomes fun, meaningful, productive, and often profitable. Brené Brown, author of *Daring Greatly*, refers to this as living wholeheartedly.

Darla Englemann, a mentor who traveled alongside me on my journey for nearly two decades, says, "If you can't do it with heart, then it's not yours to do." I know that when my "Why" is engaged, I'm enthusiastic and passionate, and when I'm occasionally buying into the "why nots," more effort is needed to accomplish any task.

Showing up in our own story—being present with it and embracing our mission—takes courage. It's a ride to be enjoyed and not feared, and it requires dancing at our edges, taking risks to step out of our comfort zone. Often, we're brought to our knees before we're truly able to rise above the limitations and expectations we've accepted from others. It's a journey—one that is for the warrior—not for the ego-driven coward who merely is looking for accolades. Humility and vulnerability are a must.

At times we think it might be easier to play small, to hide, and, for a time, it might be. But the soul's calling is much more powerful. It never goes away. Listening to it brings us energy, peace, and a sense of excitement. Denying it—resisting our calling—is a path into the abyss of despair. We then look to food, alcohol, and unhealthy sexual partners to soothe our agony. Those outlets only increase it. At different points in my life, I've tried just about anything to ignore my "Why." Thankfully, its hold over me is stronger than any "why not."

While both men and women may fall under the spell of the master narrative, women often have the most difficult time extracting themselves from it. With practice, many women are changing. It takes practice and a community of support to stand by us when we falter. With role models such as Brené Brown, Cheryl Sandberg, Angela Ahrendts, Ariana Huffington, and Oprah, more women will

At times when we think it might be easier to play small, to hide, and for a time it might be. But the soul's calling is much more powerful. It never goes away. Listening to it brings us energy, peace, and a sense of excitement.

likely become the stars in their own stories—sooner rather than later—particularly if we are on the lookout for those who can shine a light on our path.

One of my favorite role models in the media hails from *Madam Secretary*, Téa Leoni, playing Secretary of State Elizabeth McCord. She reminds women of the importance of being willing to stand in our power, even at the risk of being dismissed or challenged. Furthermore, she shows us how we can be powerful and fully grounded in our sensuality and sexuality at the same time—and be valued for that. Her husband, Henry McCord, played by Tim Daly, is a fine example of a man not threatened by a powerful woman partner. Both can be described, using David Deida's terms, as evolved.

Author of *The Way of the Superior Man: A Spiritual Guide to Mastering the Challenges of Women, Work, and Sexual Desire,* Deida describes an evolved man as "purposeful, confident, and directed, living his chosen way of life with deep integrity—and he is sensitive, spontaneous, and spiritually alive, with a heart-commitment to discovering and living his deepest truth." He is living his "Why."

An evolved woman can be described in the same way. Women can learn to be more confident and protective of our gifts, unwilling to buy into the stories written for us by other people. We can learn to expect to be honored for what we bring to the table. We can learn to unite our natural tendencies to nurture and heal with committing to our purpose, our mission, and our stories—our "Why."

Courageous Conversations with Ourselves

Whether we are a male or female leader—or an aspiring leader—we all have the power to step more fully into our "Why." It takes what poet and philosopher David Whyte, author of *Crossing the Unknown Sea: Work as a Pilgrimage of Identity*, refers to as a "courageous conversation with oneself." The time for busyness must be set aside, and we must enter that uncomfortable liminal space—the space where we've left the shore of what no longer works for us and we cannot yet see what awaits us on the distant shore. It's the space of the unknown—sometimes referred to as the dark night of the soul.

Whyte says, "To have faith in the night means we have a secret loyalty to things other than those that are so slavishly celebrated by the others in the day… Beneath the surface of our morning commute we realize that something is taking us away in the opposite direction, that wants not just another job, but another life."

The way we create another life is by listening to that still voice within us that draws our attention to that which matters most to us. For me, the small voice calls me to my computer to write down those words that are swirling inside me that I know others wish to hear or express themselves. Other times I'm creating personal and professional development programs, using the platforms of nature, writing, and fly fishing as a mirror to what's occurring in our daily activities—where those "why not" stories have reign over our lives.

As I do so, I'm aware of another voice usually appearing alongside of the voice of wisdom. That is the voice of the stories I've lived in the past. Whenever I feel the remnants of those rise to the surface as a ripple of fear or resistance, I pause and look them straight in the eye. I ask myself, "What is it that I need to be doing now?" Often, I need to rest, reset, relax. Then I'm able to face my demons and comfort the fearful inner child, assuring her that I (we) will survive. And if one tribe kicks me out, another one awaits.

To show up more fully in my story, I make a daily commitment to myself and my dreams. I schedule time for my writing and exercise, before rushing out the door to teach or into video meetings with my clients. I commit to "turning pro." I feel I have no choice. If I choose not to, I may still inhabit the planet, but I will be merely a shell going through the motions, living the stories created by those too afraid to follow their own calling, too afraid to step into their own greatness.

Choosing whom we spend time with is important. Jim Rohn says, "We're the average of the five people we spend the most time with." I've eliminated the chaos in my life by avoiding the energy vampires. I've created stability by tending to my environment, keeping order in my house, and clearing up distractions and unfinished business. And even when other people's drama may rear its head, I'm less likely to be thrown off by it because I've strengthened my core—emotionally, physically, and spiritually.

I take care of my body, mind, and spirit by practicing yoga, meditating, and getting the sleep I need to remain sharp and in-tune with my intuition. I live a disciplined lifestyle that allows for enough flexibility to keep me from feeling rigid.

Spending time in nature is a must as well. I hike, either alone or with family and friends, in and around my town or when traveling. I also fly fish, communing with my inner wisdom as I "wet my line" in the mountains of Colorado or wherever my travels find me.

Mostly, I've learned to say no—no to that which doesn't feel loving to me—whether it's a request from a colleague, a new client that isn't a good fit, or even helping a family member.

No matter what I'm doing, I'm always dancing at my edge—having that courageous conversation with myself, asking where I'm holding back, where I've become too comfortable—and what I need to be doing to "Show up, Be Present, and Do as I'm Called to Do"—to be a pro.

Pressfield says, "Turning pro is not for everyone. We have to be a little crazy to do it, or even to want to do it. In many ways the passage chooses us; we don't choose it. We simply have no alternative. What we get when we turn pro, is we find our power. We find our will and our voice and we find our self-respect. We become who we always were but had, until then, been afraid to embrace it to live it out."

When we step into our story, into our leadership, we become who we are meant to be. How could it be otherwise? As the Sufi poet Hafiz says: "All the talents of God are within you."

Our unique talents are meant to be expressed in this world. It's our "Why."

Reflection

What is Your "Why"?

_____

_____

_____

What "Why Nots" are holding you back?

_____

_____

_____

Suggestion

Each morning ask: How will I commit to myself today? Write down three ways you will honor yourself—whether it's to get in bed by ten, talk a walk at lunch, or spend fifteen minutes doing something that you simply love doing, even if it's the art of doing nothing, what the Dutch refer to as "Niksen."

If you'd like to explore your "Why," and become unstuck from your "why nots," send me an email to set up a strategy session: kathy@kathysparrow.com

Kathy Sparrow is a writing and publishing consultant, message strategist, award-winning author, speaker, and university professor. She holds a Master's degree in English with an emphasis in literature and cultural studies. An expert in narrative theory, she assists individuals in embracing change, discovering more about themselves, and expressing themselves with confidence, awareness, and courage using the tools of writing, fly fishing, and intentional conversation.

She is known as a "behind-the-scenes secret weapon" to leaders in many fields. Her chapter, "It's All in the Cast—A Fly Fisher's Guide to Leadership" appears in *The Innovators: Revolutionary Ideas from Today's Consulting Leaders*. She explains how fly fishing acts as a mirror for life and is a tool to develop confidence in self-expression at work, in love, and with family and friends.

Her novel, *The Whispered Teachings of Grandmother Trout,* is touted as the feminine version of Norman Maclean's *A River Runs Through It.*

Kathy trains extensively in the realm of leadership, with a focus on self-leadership. She studied with Jack Canfield in his Success Principles Train the Trainer program and served several years on his assisting team. She is a Certified Canfield Trainer in the Canfield Methodologies, a Be Well Lead Well Pulse® Guide, and also Master RIM® facilitator—which is an evolutionary modality designed to help individuals overcome limitations and self-sabotaging behaviors often associated with trauma.

Kathy is very active in Project Healing Waters Fly Fishing, serving as Media Lead for the Colorado Springs region, as well as Mentor and Assistant Trip Lead. The nationwide organization offers fly fishing excursions and instruction to disabled veterans and disabled active duty military.

Her hobbies are yoga, hiking, and fly fishing. Her website is www.kathysparrow.com

CHAPTER 2

Conscious Leadership
Leading Others by First Leading Yourself

by Pete Winiarski

In the corporate world, there are enormous expectations from the board, the executive team, your boss, and your customers. You probably have a global supply chain and occasional supply issues. You have a shrinking resource pool with the pressure to constantly cut costs. There is a shorter time frame within which you have to deliver your results. All of this can hamper your confidence as a leader.

Entrepreneurs and small business owners also have huge challenges. The pressure to compete is often about survival. Building the right team to support you as you move from a small company to a larger one, and profitably manage the growth that you experience, can be a daunting task.

In all the above cases, these huge challenges are often managed through brute force. As a business leader, you work longer, harder, and do whatever it takes, because you want to succeed. So does your team.

The problem is this is not a sustainable way to act as a leader. You risk burning out as an individual and you risk burning out your team. I have experienced this myself and know firsthand how this type of leadership can affect everyone near and dear to you and negatively impact your body, mind, and spirit.

Here's some great news: you can be a more effective leader and achieve your team and company goals with less stress and more personal and team satisfaction.

Imagine this:

- You love your job and your company, and you look forward to work each day.
- You have clarity and confidence that what you do fits into your higher purpose and adds fuel to your passion.
- You get rockstar results.
- You trust your team, and they love working with you.
- Your team has bought into your vision.
- You are proud of how well your team gels. The team cohesion and camaraderie has a huge positive impact on everyone with whom you all interact. It is infectious and reflects your great results.
- Even when you do choose to work long hours, you are energized and excited at the end of each day.

This is all possible for you right now, despite the huge challenges you face as a business leader.

Choose to Get Off the Path to Burnout

Back when I was an executive in corporate America, our company had a great track record of solid performance and high margins, and we were often asked to cover for other business units that were going to miss their financial targets. As you know, in the corporate world you are simply not allowed to miss your financial commitments. Enter the "go-get."

The go-get was the target you had to hit to cover the other business's shortfalls. The problem with how we used the go-get was that it was a target that exceeded all of the plans and budgets that we had put in place and was usually somewhat of a last-minute request. We had to find a way to squeeze more results out of our business in order to hit that go-get. By the way, we were not in a company turn-around situation with the risk of going belly up—the go-get was required to deliver financial expectations to Wall Street.

It seemed that every quarter we were asked to hit some huge stretch numbers. Now, if you've been through any of my public seminars on goal achievement or workshops on Strategic Goal Deployment™, then you know *some* stretch is good. The problem the go-gets created is that in order to hit these numbers, we had to do things that compromised the systems and processes that delivered solid results. We relied on brute force in order to hit the number. You can see how this regular grind contributed to eventually burning out my team and me.

Burnout is a huge risk in the brute force model. Despite my efforts to keep things positive, key resources began to quit, and recruiting replacements became a major time sink. I wasn't enjoying what my job had become and was struggling to keep remaining team members on task. What started as a fun job turned into, well, dread. I soon left the corporate world to start my own business, Win Enterprises, LLC.

Shortly after forming Win, I ramped up my investment in personal and professional development. I became more self-aware, tapped into my higher purpose, and noticed that while I sometimes worked my butt off, I loved what I was doing and it just didn't feel like "work" the way that it had in the past. I realized how critical this alignment was as I built a hugely successful consulting business, wrote an international best-selling book, accepted invitations to be a suitably well-paid keynote speaker for a variety of organizations, created a unique and highly effective coaching model, and enjoyed working with my many diverse clients.

My team at Win Enterprises, LLC is great. They buy into my vision, and we all have fun. Sure, we sometimes work pretty hard, like when we prepare for a major event, such as a book launch, workshop, or major client project, but we know how to inject some downtime to recharge our batteries. This is the way that it can work for you as well.

Notice What Might be Missing for You

Looking back at my corporate experience, I now realize that I was missing some critical elements as a leader. Despite my wealth of knowledge and experience, I was somehow incomplete. Until I was able to fill these voids, I would not be able to lead in the most optimal way. I had to learn to lead myself before I could more effectively lead others.

To effectively lead myself, I had to recognize that some of my beliefs simply would no longer serve me well. For example, I believed there was a separation required between personal development and business. Business (at least in a corporate environment) is stiff and impersonal, right? What I recognize now is that everything in personal development translates into the business world. When business leaders figure this out, they become way more effective. Personal success methods, like visualizing goals, writing clear action plans, and meditating are all effective for teams and business leaders.

Another belief was that I had to work really hard to be successful and get results, with great personal sacrifice, stress, and long hours to pound through whatever my projects were so that I could meet expectations. Sometimes those expectations were from myself, but often they were from other people. Typically, beliefs like these come from deeper fears that we all have. We want to do a good job and we want to be perceived as a committed hard worker. The trick here is about alignment. If you are not aligned with your higher purpose and your passion, you will soon burn out.

What I now know to be true is that as leaders build a more conscious awareness of themselves, they can become more effective. They get great personal results in a way that helps them to manage stress and helps them experience more inner peace and joy in the process. They display a higher level of self-confidence that translates to the other people around them. Leaders who develop this higher conscious awareness of self then inspire others and build a following.

Leaders also apply the same process to their interactions with other people. They become more aware of the needs, the drivers and motivators, the skills, and the capabilities of the people around them: their team, their peers, their customers, their suppliers, and their bosses. This all allows them to engage in a way that maximizes performance and achieves greater results.

The Win Holistic Transformation Model™

I created the Win Holistic Transformation Model™ to describe how business leaders can transform their companies and results. The graphic below illustrates this model:

Transformation begins with clarity about the results that you seek and a recognition of the magnitude of change that is possible. Next, you want to have organizational alignment and a clear sense of the company's Purpose, Vision, Mission, and Goals. In order to achieve transformational results, there are a number of elements to put in place—the five points of the star—to ensure you efficiently and effectively make progress.

- *Strategy Engagement Execution*™ *(SEE*™*)* is our proprietary process of using Strategic Goal Deployment™ so you can prioritize your company's strategic goals and ensure that your organization is focused and aligned on the right actions, and then engaging the organization to execute the strategies.

- The *Science of Success* gets into the mindsets and the processes that are proven to help you and your teams create great results.

- *Lean Thinking* is the set of philosophies and tools that help you drive operational improvement and efficiency in how work gets done.

- *Conscious Leadership* is how you can lead in the most effective way.

- *The Winning Team* is how you develop your team and then utilize team-based approaches to get things done.

All of your company's activity occurs within your company's *culture*. Your culture has the power to accelerate your progress or knock you off track, so you want to actively design it to support the direction and method of how you want things to work in your company. As you implement the elements of the star, you will shape your culture, reinforce your transformation efforts, and sustain the results you get. Because culture is the sum of all your employees' beliefs, thoughts, and behaviors, the element that can impact your culture most quickly, as you shape other people's beliefs, thoughts, and behaviors, is *Conscious Leadership*.

> *What I now know to be true is that as leaders build a more conscious awareness of themselves, they can become more effective.*

Now that you have the context of the larger framework, let's go deeper into *Conscious Leadership*, so you can learn how to maximize the impact of your personal leadership for you, your team, and your company.

Conscious Leadership

Conscious Leadership builds on traditional concepts of leadership and is about driving transformational change: for yourself, for others, and ultimately for your business.

To be effective as leaders, all leaders must know the boundaries of their responsibilities and the expectations of their team. They have a vision of where they're going and communicate that vision well among their people. They build a team of the right resources, so they have the skills to get the job done. These are the "non-negotiable" items that all leaders need to have in place.

Conscious Leadership

Conscious of Self	Conscious of Others
1. Are centered and grounded	1. Are humble
2. Have clarity in their life	2. Are trustworthy
3. Are self-aware	3. Act equally as coaches, mentors, and students
4. Are introspective and curious	4. Are engaged with and committed to developing teams

Conscious Leadership is the next level of leadership beyond the obvious nonnegotiable items we already know. Conscious leaders operate with two fundamental elements—they are called *Conscious of Self* and *Conscious of Others*

Conscious leaders begin by building a conscious awareness of themselves and possess these four characteristics:

1. Are centered and grounded
2. Have clarity in their life
3. Are self-aware
4. Are introspective and curious

Additionally, conscious leaders build a conscious awareness of others around them, including their teams, their peers, and other people in their sphere of influence. When conscious of others, they possess four additional characteristics:

1. Are humble
2. Are trustworthy
3. Act equally as coaches, mentors, and students
4. Are engaged with and committed to developing teams

When leaders are conscious of self, they inspire others by their personal results and style. When leaders are conscious of others, they build followership and create a team that is capable of great performance and positively transforming company results.

Conscious of Self Characteristics

Now let's delve a little deeper into the *Conscious of Self* characteristics that conscious leaders possess.

1. *Centered and grounded.* When leaders are centered and grounded, they are aware of their strengths and weaknesses. They know what they are passionate about. They are clear on their vision. They understand what's important and critical and are aware of items that arise that are unimportant. For many of you, it's the unimportant—or non-critical—items that lure you off track (the next shiny object). Centered and grounded leaders stay focused and have a high level of self-confidence, which they exude in their words and actions.

2. *Clarity in their life.* Your brain desires clarity to actively guide you on your journey and help you achieve your goals. When you are clear about your purpose, your vision, and your direction, it's far easier to march toward them in an effortless way. In the absence of clarity, you risk bouncing around like a ball in a pinball machine—your direction can be shifted by the bumpers of life.

   Consider these questions:

   • What is your personal vision, and how do you want your life to work?

   • What are you passionate about?

   • As a business leader, how do you leverage your passion?

   • Do your goals align with your vision and desired experiences?

You will find that when you align with your higher purpose and vision and consciously choose to find ways to live your passion, you will be more fulfilled. This clarity can act as guidance for your decisions and the direction in which you choose to go.

3. *Self-aware.* Think of the beliefs and values that guide you, drive you, and define who you are. Are you even aware that some of your beliefs may no longer serve you and could be replaced by more positive and empowering beliefs? What are your strengths? What are your weaknesses? How do you utilize your strengths and capitalize on the gifts that you've been given? Do you build a team around you to cover for those things that either you don't like to do or that you're simply not good at or that you are good at but require a LOT of your energy to do? You can build your plans around these answers to maximize your impact as a business leader and as a person.

4. *Introspective and curious.* From an introspective standpoint, what processes do you have in place to enable you to trust yourself and to "check in" with your intuition, as guided by your higher purpose? Introspective activities include meditation, journaling, prayer, contemplation, and any other activity to help clear your mind of the mental chatter. It's a skill to clear your mind of clutter, get it to relax, and become quiet enough to hear the whisper of your intuition. Remember, your intuition has the ability to guide you through your biggest challenges, so learn to pay attention.

Curiosity refers to being unattached to the outcomes and the details of how things happen. When things don't unfold exactly as you thought they might, approach those situations from a place of curiosity. Let go of your need to be in control and allow your inquisitive nature to find the message for you. This works extremely well when you trust that everything happens for a reason and your higher purpose can, and will, serve to guide you.

Conscious of Others Characteristics

Conscious leaders are also aware of those around them and how they affect others. Let's review each of these characteristics.

1. *Humble.* Humble does not mean that you are weak. It means that you've dropped your ego, which can actually make you stronger in the eyes of others around you. As a humble business leader, you give credit to others. You are open-minded, and you can accept personal responsibility and act in a way that's accountable. You seek out feedback with genuine interest about the answer, and you give feedback to others in a way that creates a team atmosphere and builds relationships that foster camaraderie.

2. *Trustworthy.* Trust is an important characteristic in any organization and relationship. As a business leader, unless your team and the others around you can trust who you are, that you'll do the right thing, and that you have their back, you cannot achieve an optimum level of teamwork and performance. In order to build trust, you must first be trustworthy. Trustworthy means that you behave in a way that people know what to expect from you and want to work with you. Remember, that which you want is what you should give. As you trust your team members, you build their skill and their confidence. When you demonstrate that you have their back, even when they don't perform exactly the way you want, that builds deeper trust.

3. *Coaches, mentors, and students.* There's a lot of dialogue about leadership and that moving from manager to leader involves becoming more of a coach or mentor to others. At risk of sounding cliché, I agree that this is important as a leadership characteristic, but what do we really mean? Do we mean that we all need to become certified coaches who can diagnose deeper personal and emotional challenges that people on your team may have? Does it mean that we need to become skilled at helping people to rewire their beliefs, or to even resolve internal conflict that they've been carrying since they were young children? No, I'm not saying that—but I do think it's important to build an awareness of elements that make people unique and that motivate or drive us to be who we are and to perform at our best.

My message to you is to understand the people on your team. Help them to work through their challenges and learn the processes to make them better and perform at a higher level. The aspect of being a student means that you continue to engage your curiosity, observe, and learn from those around you. It includes asking for feedback and ideas, and being open to the possibility that the ideas of others can contribute to great results.

4. *Engaged with and committed to developing teams.* Creating teams of people to solve problems and implement new ideas is clearly a more powerful approach than letting individuals attempt this on their own. There's a better flow of ideas when team members collaborate and inject their own individual perspectives. Leaders who recognize the power of teamwork invest in helping teams go through the natural phases of

team development and reside in high performance for as long as possible. Personally engaging with teams, clarifying your vision, sharing your expectations, and holding frequent progress review meetings and problem-solving discussions can help keep the team energized and on track. Ultimately, it is the power of the team that can move your results beyond the current performance that individual effort creates.

Reference this overview of the characteristics of *Conscious Leadership* and experiment with all of them. Developing yourself as a leader is a process that takes place over time, and frankly, never really ends for a conscious leader.

As you review the Conscious of Self and Conscious of Others characteristics, you might wonder if there is a "Fast Track" way to implement them. I'm excited to share that there is indeed!

I am accredited to deliver Insights Discovery®, a psychometric evaluation based on the psychology of the Swiss psychologist Carl Jung. What you will learn—about how "attitudinal functions" impact the way you play the game of life—will be astoundingly accurate and helpful as you begin to first lead yourself and then lead others.

Conscious Leadership and the Mind, Body, Spirit Connection

As a conscious leader, you realize there is an intersection between mind, body, and spirit. When all three are working in concert, you can optimize your effectiveness.

Mind. Use your full mind, which includes the thinking part of your brain and the unconscious, or subconscious, parts of your mind. Reprogram your thinking away from the "Automatic Negative Thoughts," or ANTs, as Dr. Daniel Amen calls them, toward a more optimistic and positive outlook. Use your thoughts to shape your habits so that your unconscious mind supports you and your goals more actively.

Body. Positively impact your body as you manage your stress and energy levels. The sum of all the *Conscious Leadership* practices will keep you excited about each day, as your path and actions align with your purpose and passion and fuel your energy to keep you moving. As a conscious leader, external factors that once caused you stress are now viewed as simply peripheral events that may or may not even require your attention.

Spirit. While the idea of spirit—or spiritual guidance—may be taboo for some in the business world, intuition certainly isn't. A conscious leader knows how to trust their spirit in the form of guidance from their intuition, and does so actively each day. Rather than argue whether this insight or "intuitive hit" comes from God, Spirit, or is born from deep within your brain's unconscious realm, let's agree to recognize the power of your intuition and its role to help you. This is an "internal GPS" that, as you learn to trust it, will provide a powerful advantage for you in every area of your life.

The connection that is created between your mind, body, and spirit is there because we are complete people. Business leaders are not immune to the stresses of daily life. You have kids who have to stay home sick from school, unexpected maintenance your houses or cars require, storms that knock out power for a few days, birthday or holiday parties that you are expected to attend, spouses who want to spend more quiet time with you, or even a pandemic that causes you to work from home and change your daily lives. All these occur during our busy schedules—it's part of life. Practicing *Conscious Leadership* helps you bring awareness, balance, and peace in all areas of your life as you learn to deal with all these daily challenges and take them in stride.

Make Conscious Leadership Your Leadership Model

Actively study and be attentive to all the characteristics of *Conscious Leadership* and how you integrate them in your life. Here are some thoughts of how to make them your natural leadership style.

Conscious of Self means that you embark on self-improvement and that each day is a new opportunity for you to try new strategies, notice what is working, and be at your best. Carve out some personal time every day for yourself. You might find that the first hour of your day is best, before you get distracted. Practice your introspective activities, like meditating, journaling, reading, or exercising before you become available for other people and your public agenda.

If you schedule one or two personal development seminars or workshops each year, you will deepen your perspectives. These might be designed for business leaders, or for individuals—both types will benefit you. Develop daily routines that align with the type of leader you want to be. The daily routine and process I describe in my #1 International Best Seller, *Act Now! A Daily Action Log for Achieving Your Goals in 90 Days*, is a perfect way to get started. Visit www.DailyActionLog.com for more information and resources. You will soon find that all of the *Conscious of Self* characteristics will create improvements for you.

As you continue to work on yourself, you actually boost your ability to lead others. The reason I suggest to lead others by first leading yourself, is that by practicing *Conscious of Self* characteristics, you naturally begin to develop *Conscious of Others* characteristics.

To better understand *Conscious of Others*, think of someone that you have encountered during your career who was not humble or trustworthy, perhaps an ex-boss or a peer, and recall their behavior. Notice their empty promises, the way they were clearly in it for themselves, their arrogance, or how they would get results by stepping on others rather than supporting and helping people succeed. Do you have a clear picture in your mind? Good! Now, don't do that! Replace that picture with one that describes who you want to be as a leader, and make this new picture your normal practice.

Seven Tips to Get You Started

1. One of the biggest tips I can offer you is to **engage your team in your personal journey**. They will appreciate your effort, support you, and make progress themselves. For example, I have an event designed for business leaders called *Your Best Year Ever*, where people begin to think of their business leadership role differently as they gain clarity about their higher purpose and goals, and then learn strategies to achieve them. The attendees at this event include founders, CEOs, executives, small business owners, and entrepreneurs.

Many of the managers who attend this event bring people from their teams to engage them right from the start. It's an awesome experience when these entire teams embark on the journey together.

2. A second tip for you is to **assess your level of *conscious leadership*.** I invite you to take the *Conscious Leadership Assessment,* which can be found at https://completebusinesstransformation.com/win-conscious-leadership/. Once you have a sense of how you measure up to the *Conscious Leadership* characteristics, you can decide actions that will further develop your abilities as a conscious leader.

3. Third, **reach out to my team and ask about taking the Insights Discovery® evaluator** and going through our process to use that information to accelerate your *Conscious Leadership* characteristics. We will help you become more self-aware, and expand your *Conscious of Self* characteristics, then support you to put *Conscious of Others* characteristics in place, especially as you engage with and develop your teams.

4. Fourth, **work with a coach or Executive Mentor** who can tailor approaches and guide you to break through your biggest barriers.

5. Next, **commit to at least one personal or professional development seminar or workshop each year.** I've practiced this myself since 2006. I've worked with a variety of personal coaches and have averaged over seventeen days a year in seminars or workshops as a student between 2006 and 2014 (yes, I actually calculated this!). The difference in both my

results and well-being has been remarkable and has provided a huge ROI for me. I expect the same for you.

6. Next, **share these principles with someone else.** When you teach others, you deepen your own knowledge. Plus, you now have a buddy with whom you can go through your *Conscious Leadership* experience, and can support each other.

7. Finally, choose one characteristic of *Conscious Leadership,* and **decide three actions that you will take** right now to improve this characteristic for you. The important thing is taking action and committing to practicing *Conscious Leadership.*

Insights Discovery® Accreditation Training Materials,© 2013-2018. Insights Discovery® is a product of Insights Learning & Development Limited, Dundee, Scotland. Insights Discovery® Accreditation materials include four workbooks by these titles: *The Insights Discovery® Theory Practitioner Guide, Preparing to Deliver Insights Discovery® Practitioner Guide, Delivering Insights Discovery® Practitioner Guide,* and *Applying Insights Discovery® Practitioner Guide.*

Pete Winiarski helps business leaders transform themselves, their teams, and their companies. He is the CEO of Win Enterprises, LLC, which has created over $100 million in value for clients through its Consulting and Executive Mentoring programs. Previously, he was an executive in corporate America and senior leader in consulting companies including McKinsey and Company, The George Group, and Accenture.

Pete is a recognized thought leader in business and personal transformation, and he has written multiple books, including the #1 International Best-Selling book, *Act Now! A Daily Action Log for Achieving Your Goals in 90 Days* and *Stop Wasting Money on the Wrong Consultant: How to Pick the Right Consultant to Create Huge Profits and Long-Term ROI*. He also created the *Win Holistic Transformation Model*TM as the framework by which a company could guide their path to achieving transformational results. Part of this model includes *Conscious Leadership*, which is the topic of this chapter. Pete has also appeared frequently on TV as a business expert and as a goal achievement expert.

Contact Pete's Team Now

For media appearances, keynote speaking, consulting, or Executive Mentoring support, visit: www.CompleteBusinessTransformation.com or call the office at +1 860.651.6859

Discover if you are a Conscious Leader

Take the assessment to see if you're a Conscious Leader. Visit: https://completebusinesstransformation.com/win-conscious-leadership/

Ask About Accelerating Your Conscious Leadership Using Insights Discovery®

Email support@CompleteBusinessTransformation.com or call our office directly at +1 860 651.6859.

Catch the Latest Podcast

Listen to: The Business Results Program on iTunes: http://bit.ly/businessresultsradio

Read the Latest Blog

Read the blog at: https://completebusinesstransformation.com

CHAPTER 3

Powering Personal Energy
The "kW" of Energized Leadership

by Nathalie Osborn

When I was first asked to write this chapter, I was excited about the opportunity. I thought it would be easy and that I had my message on leadership all "figured out." I'd had a successful career, easily earned six figures, and was a well-respected leader in the energy industry. My experiences included launching one of the largest solar incentive programs in the world, sitting on the boards of national organizations, and implementing over $500M in energy efficiency and renewable energy projects.

As I began to write, I started to question what leadership message I would share, because there was more to the story. I was a successful leader in my industry, yet I hadn't been completely happy. I'd had a challenging couple of years, felt vulnerable, and wondered if I had anything to contribute to this book. Unlike my co-authors, my background was in energy, not leadership development. What did energy have to do with leadership? What was I going to share about leadership, especially when I felt this way?

The more I questioned myself, the more I realized my journey—my message about leadership, specifically energizing personal leadership—was the story I needed to share. After all, personal energy management is the foundation of leadership, and perhaps my expertise in the energy industry wasn't that far off the mark!

My journey starts with my transition from the energy industry to the training industry. In my quest to have it all and to energize my life, I chose to shift gears in my career. I was confident and had always managed change well in the past. Based on this history, I just "knew" I would find a way to succeed. I did what so many passionate entrepreneurs do: I quit my six-figure job to follow my passion. Instead of making buildings more energy efficient, I would focus on the energy of people and organizations. I was personally energized and ready to ignite my new career.

I moved from San Diego to the Pacific Northwest for a fresh start, where I spent a year "kick-starting" my business. I loved the freedom of managing my own time, creating new consulting products and developing training services. Networking and marketing my business provided exciting opportunities to meet new people; however, I wasn't making much money. I was living primarily off my savings, and while energized, I still wasn't completely happy.

So I moved back "home" to the Midwest, closer to my family whom I had missed, back to a larger support network, and back to a steady paycheck. I took an entry-level job with an international training and development company at a fraction of the pay I knew I was worth. I told myself this sacrifice would be worth it. While it wasn't my own company, I was still pursuing my dream, working in the training industry, and powering people—instead of buildings—to become more energy efficient. I loved the company's content, and with confidence in my proven track record, I once again "knew" I could find opportunities to advance and succeed within the organization.

But things didn't go according to my plan, and the organization didn't embrace my dream. It didn't matter that I topped the performance scoreboards for my position or how passionate I was about their content. It didn't matter that I had spent my evenings, weekends, and my own personal time going through the company's coursework to improve my performance in my current role and prepare myself for more advanced roles within the company. In the end, I realized my managers didn't see my potential or support my desire to grow into an advanced role.

I'd hit a roadblock, and I was crushed. Yet, I also learned a valuable lesson: I had undersold myself. I had done so by convincing myself the sacrifice in accepting an entry-level role, and a significant cut in pay, would in the end be worth it, because I was "getting my foot in the door" in a new industry.

In reality, what I had done, was told the organization I would accept less than what I was worth and also implied I didn't have the necessary skills needed for the advanced roles, even though I was already well-qualified. Unfamiliar with the energy industry, how my skills were transferrable, and my successful track record, they had accepted my offer. My new managers saw me exactly at the level at which I sold myself. I'd sold myself short, and I had to take responsibility for what I had done. Unfortunately, so many of us, especially women, often do the same.

According to Katty Kay and Claire Shipman, authors of *The Confidence Code: The Science and Art of Self-Assurance—What Women Should Know,* "In study after study, the data confirms what we instinctively know: underqualified and underprepared men don't think twice about leaning in. Overqualified and over prepared, too many women still hold back."

While I'd had my fair share of ups and downs in life, selling myself short appeared to compound my problems. My confidence was at an all-time low, and for the first time in my life, I felt really lost. I always tended to have a sense of inner confidence, and now this inner confidence was tested. Unlike the past, I felt I wasn't succeeding at what I had put my mind to, and I didn't understand why. These emotions were all so new for me.

I'd lost my way, and I'd lost my energy. Contemplating what had worked for me in the past, I realized that my success in the energy industry had always been charged by my passion for personal growth and goal setting, which included knowing who I was, what I wanted, and why I wanted it. I had strayed from this path and let my ego take charge. I was depleted, and I had to find a way to renew, refuel, and recharge my personal energy.

In our modern world where we are plugged in 24/7, it is not uncommon for many of us to be tired, burned out, and running on empty. We have a "human energy" crisis, and it's costing us, personally and professionally, hours of time and millions of dollars. In our personal lives, it's costing us our happiness, fulfillment, and livelihood. In our companies, where people are the fuel of our organizations, we're shorting the circuit on high performance and high productivity by running on empty.

Our capacity to be happy, productive, and successful is driven by how well we are able to renew, refuel, and recharge our own personal energy. Leadership is about harnessing our own human energy and becoming leaders in our lives. It's about learning how to ignite our passions to fuel our own happiness and enrich our own lives.

I believe we need to become energized leaders who are focused on positively managing our personal energy. Energized leaders who understand high performance and high productivity in our lives are not sustainable when we continue to short circuit our own human energy. Leaders who find ways to unleash their own personal energy—to power and capture it—fueling their full potential first, which in turn, encourages others around them to do the same. Energized corporate leaders who understand and realize that people are the creative force, the current, and the fuel of our organizations, and personally powered employees will positively fuel highly productive and profitable companies.

> *Our capacity to be productive, to be successful, and to be happy is driven by how well we are able to renew, refuel, and recharge our own personal energy.*

While serving as Senior Vice President at Apple, Angela Ahrendts said, "Human energy single-handedly has the power to unite and transform organizations." As an energized leader, she's right!

In the energy industry, I work with companies to identify ways to save energy in their buildings and generate their own renewable power. By saving energy and generating their own power, they are managing their kilowatts, or "kW" more efficiently.

I realized my success and my self-confidence are fueled from within when I power my personal energy, my own "kW." A "kW" driven by clarity in knowing who I am, what I want, and why I am driven toward my goals. We can all energize our personal power, our own "kW," which can be self-generated in three key ways:

- *k*nowing *W*ho • *k*nowing *W*hat • *k*nowing *W*hy

The First "kW" - Knowing Who

The first step in powering your personal energy and becoming an energized leader is *knowing who* you are and embracing it. Energized leaders know who they are, and they step into their power with true conviction. With a high sense of self-awareness, they are confident in their strengths, understanding of their weaknesses, and fearlessly authentic. They are humble, genuine, and grateful. Energized leaders are crystal clear: they know who they are at their core, and they know who they need to become in order to accomplish their goals, enrich their lives, and be happy.

Energized leaders focus on developing their own character, honoring their words, and keeping their commitments. They aren't afraid to take responsibility and hold themselves accountable. Energized leaders are not perfect. They know they will at times fumble and understand that fumbling is part of the process of chasing their goals and energizing their lives. They aren't afraid to be transparent about not having all the answers or acknowledging their mistakes.

Relentless about ongoing self-improvement, energized leaders commit to continuously learning, taking action, and adjusting their strategies based on feedback. Tony Schwartz, CEO of The Energy Project, says, "Self-awareness is a competitive advantage." While true, taking the time for honest self-reflection and making a commitment to a greater sense of self-awareness isn't an easy exercise. Self-awareness calls for being honest with yourself. It also requires you to be willing to ask for and listen to the feedback you are receiving, both positive and negative.

When I undervalued and undersold myself to the training company, I strayed from my own conviction of *knowing who* I was and *knowing what* I was worth. To shift, I needed to pause, self-reflect, and renew my personal "kW." When I summoned the courage to dive deep, I came face-to-face with my own insecurities. I became aware of my fear of failure, my overconfidence in certain situations, and my need to control an outcome—like how I "knew" I would be able to advance within the training company on my own timeline!

The engineer in myself needed to admit that I didn't have to solve all the problems, have all the answers, or do it all by myself. Yet, what frightened me most was discovering a deep-rooted limiting belief that was holding me back: *I could either be broke pursuing a career that I loved or be wealthy in a passionless career.* To recharge and grow, I needed to change that belief and rewire my thinking. While it wasn't easy, acknowledging the actions and mindset that were holding me back provided clarity on what I needed to change and who I needed to become to refuel my personal power.

Making the time to really get to know who we are at our core is also one of the greatest gifts we can give ourselves. In asking myself, "Who am I?", I was also able to remind myself of my accomplishments, strengths, and talents. By asking others I trusted and listening to their feedback, especially when it stung, I was able to shine a light on my weaknesses and opportunities for growth. Refueling my personal energy included revising a personal mission statement I had created years earlier and making a list of what I enjoyed doing, both personally and professionally. Most importantly, my self-reflection involved learning how to have more patience with myself and more gratitude for my life. In refueling my personal "kW," I was able to reconnect with *knowing who* I am, recharge my inner confidence, and step back into my power.

By taking responsibility for renewing my personal energy and powering my "kW," it became crystal clear that I had run away from who I really needed to be—an energized leader in the energy industry! By returning to the industry, I didn't have to give up my dreams of energizing people and organizations. Instead, I could make it an "inside job," applying these skills to fuel an even greater difference within the energy industry where I already thrived.

Within organizations, energized leaders know that personally energized people powerfully and positively charge successful companies. By knowing who they are and understanding their own weaknesses, energized leaders know who to surround themselves with and know who they need on their team. They are clear about what skills they bring to the table and why they need certain individuals on their team to contribute where they fall short. Energized leaders ask questions like:

- "Who needs to be on my team?"
- "Who do I need to collaborate or partner with?"
- "Who has the necessary skills to support accomplishing this goal?"

As Jim Collins, author of *Good to Great* said, "They know who to put in the right seats on the bus."

Even with the right team, effective leadership is not about exercising power over people—it's about giving people the opportunity, support, and resources to power themselves. An energized leader wisely chooses to fuel their personal energy and ignite their "kW" first, which energizes others around them to do the same.

Fueling your personal energy by *knowing who* you are is an unstoppable force. It takes great courage to acknowledge and share our authentic selves with the world. It means wearing the good, the bad, and the ugly openly on our sleeves and owning all of who we are. Ralph Waldo Emerson encouraged, "If you want to be a power in the world, then be yourself."

kW Power Up: Energizing Knowing Who

1. Take a moment and think about who you are at your core. Silent your mind and take a few deep breaths, and ask yourself:
   - Who am I?
   - What do I enjoy doing?
   - What don't I enjoy doing?

- What are my strengths?
- What are my weaknesses?
- How might I be holding myself back?

2. Take note of your answers, and notice what you may need to improve to accomplish your goals and enrich your life. Be honest with yourself. Ask family members and friends that you trust for feedback. Listen to the feedback—especially when it stings. This typically means it has sparked something within you that you may need to acknowledge or address.

3. Take note of the people you spend your time with, and reflect:

- Do they support your goals?
- Do they add value to your life?
- Do they energize you?
- Do they have valuable skills that you need yet may not have?

4. Consider creating a personal mission statement or mantra to fuel yourself. Commit to making time for self-reflection, to continuously renew, refuel, and recharge who you are, and support your personal growth.

The Second "kW" - Knowing What

The second step to powering your personal energy as an energized leader is *knowing what* makes you happy and what you want to achieve in your life. Energized leaders know what they want to accomplish, and they develop a clear vision for each of their goals. They focus on the end in mind, they know what it will look like when their goal is achieved and, even more importantly, what it will feel like once they have succeeded.

By taking the time to visualize accomplishing their goals, living and breathing each detail, an energized leader creates a vision so powerful that it can be clearly articulated and communicated to anyone. Their passion and enthusiasm is contagious and creates an abundant energy flow which fuels, inspires, and motivates people around them to become driven to support their cause. According to fashion icon, Ralph Lauren, "When a leader has the vision and conviction that a dream can be achieved, he inspires the power and energy to get it done."

While fueled with a clear vision, an energized leader may not initially see the full path toward accomplishing their goal. However, they do know what is important—to start taking action, taking small steps forward and driving toward their goal. They know what they need to measure, consistently evaluating their progress and making adjustments, as needed along the way. In doing so, energized leaders gain great clarity on what they do, and do not, know in regard to achieving their goals. A mistake, misstep, or setback on the path toward achieving their goal is seen as an opportunity to learn and grow.

Energized leaders are humble and extremely transparent about their agendas. They aren't afraid to ask for help and seek feedback on what is or isn't working to adjust their strategy accordingly. By creating transparency around *knowing what*, they make it easier to engage others in helping them reach their goals.

Within organizations, energized leaders understand the importance of everyone on their team being in agreement on what needs to be accomplished. They involve their team members in the *knowing what* process, creating alignment and commitment to a shared vision. They create clarity around who is responsible for completing which tasks and when tasks need to be completed. They take responsibility for creating agreement on what needs to be measured, how it will be measured, and how progress will be evaluated to continuously refine the strategy. Energized leaders work to ensure everyone is crystal clear on what the organization is striving to accomplish.

In the energy industry, we refer to the "kW" of *knowing what* as benchmarking. In order to determine how to make a building more energy efficient, we measure how it currently operates by analyzing utility bills, evaluating operating procedures, and taking inventory of the building equipment. Once we understand our baseline, we set goals on how much energy we want to use and save within the building. Next, we determine what processes and projects will help us achieve our goals. As we implement our plan, we continuously measure energy use and verify savings, while making adjustments as needed for continuous improvement.

When it comes to managing our personal energy and striving toward our personal and professional goals, we can use the same process. First and foremost, we need to know what fuels us, where we're starting from, and what we want to accomplish. Once we know our "baseline," we can develop an action plan. The plan we develop for achieving our goals doesn't have to be perfect, yet, once created, we just need to get started. Upon implementing our plan, we can continuously measure our progress, evaluate our results, listen to feedback, learn new strategies, and adjust accordingly until we successfully achieve our goals.

Energized leaders are curious and want to know what inspires both themselves and the people around them. They see the energy within people as a current of unlimited potential waiting to be unleashed. They understand that in order to tap into that power, they need to clearly understand what motivates themselves and the people around them. Energized leaders want to know what people dream of accomplishing, both personally and professionally.

In team environments, they want to know what strengths each individual brings to the table and what will help support growth in areas where additional skills may need to be developed. They ask people what they need in order to feel valued, everything from what communication style they prefer, what kind of projects they enjoy, and what kind of training they need to what hours they prefer to work to be most productive.

Energized leaders want to know what kind of culture will fuel their team to sustain the productivity and profitability of their organization. They look to create positive environments that fuel collaboration and creativity. Most importantly, they engage and empower their team to support creating and sustaining that necessary culture. In an organizational culture where everyone is invested and on board with the vision, managing the team becomes easy. Energized leaders trust their employees will manage their energy and time responsibly. They have confidence that deadlines will be met, important tasks will be prioritized, and any issues or challenges that arise will be immediately addressed.

Energized leaders see the capacity that the "kW" of *knowing what* has on driving organizational goals, productivity, and profitability. They are passionate about developing organizational cultures that are able to sustain high productivity and performance over time. Furthermore, they know collaborative communication, strong systems of accountability, along with clearly defined goals and strategies are what fuels a successful organization.

Energized leaders are driven to help unleash the power of people and are committed to rewiring the circuit for human energy management. They understand the full capacity of *knowing what* and take responsibility for igniting this unlimited power. Energized leaders understand powering the "kW" of *knowing what* within themselves ignites their fuel potential, and encourages those around them to tap into their greater potential. Ultimately powering *knowing what* energizes organizational success, while also enriching and fulfilling personal lives.

kW Power Up: Energizing Knowing What

1. Take a moment to think about your personal and professional goals. Ask yourself:
   - Are you energized by your goals?
   - Are you energized by what you do?
   - Do you have a clear vision for what it looks like and feels like to accomplish your goals?
   - Do you know what baseline you're starting from?
   - Do you know what metrics you need to measure to evaluate progress toward your goals?

- Are you listening to feedback and adjusting your strategy accordingly?
- Do you know what motivates you?

2. Think about goals of your organization and its culture. Ask yourself:
   - Does your organization have clearly defined goals and a clear action plan?
   - Does your organization know what metrics you need to measure to evaluate success?
   - Is your organization responsive to feedback and adjusting strategies accordingly to fuel greater success?
   - Do you know what motivates your team, and do you have managers who know what motivates you?
   - Does your organization encourage collaboration and open communication?

The Third "kW" - Knowing Why

The energized leader's secret weapon is the third "kW" of *knowing why*. They need to know why what they're doing matters, why it's important, and why it makes a difference. The "kW" in *knowing why* runs deep and may be the most powerful of the three "kW"s. It is the personal meaning behind the vision, mission, or goal we want to achieve. It is the core purpose and driving force that makes who you are and what you want important. In *Think and Grow Rich*, author Napoleon Hill calls this force a burning desire. And it is! It's a flame that, once ignited, charges us forward.

Energized leaders understand that knowing the *why* behind who we are and what we want is the only force that will continue to drive us forward toward our goals with sustained momentum over time. It's the powerful reason that will keep us relentlessly striving, until our dreams become our reality. A purpose that energizes us and keeps us from stopping at nothing until we reach our goals.

It's our *why* that will get us up early when we would rather sleep in. Our *why* that will guide and support us with determining what is truly important to us. A powerful *why* that will help us wisely choose how to focus our energy and time on what really matters most in our lives.

Often, this *why* is fueled by something much greater than our actual goals or desires. Our *why* may be rooted in the love for our family, our faith, a passion for a particular cause, or caring for the greater good in our world. It's typically always something much greater than our ego, ourselves, our own personal agenda or need for accomplishment. An energized leader learns to manage the collective *why* of a team while balancing it with the individual *whys* of their team members.

My friend Scott, a senior director at a global defense contracting firm, is an energized leader who truly understands the power of *knowing why*. A number of years ago, he and his team were honored in Washington, DC for successfully leading a major government project, which they completed in a fraction of the typical time and within budget. If you're unfamiliar with government contracts, this was a major accomplishment!

When I asked him what contributed to the success of the project, he immediately knew it was the *why*: "First and foremost, we knew our purpose. We made it easy, we made it simple, and our purpose was clearly defined: *we were saving lives.*" To keep his team connected to their *why*, Scott and his leadership team would bring soldiers into the plant to meet with the engineers, which made their *why* even more personal. The team would use these visits to learn, listening to the soldiers' stories, clarifying their needs in the field, and getting feedback on their current designs. Their goal was to ensure they were developing the necessary life-saving products.

In regard to managing his team, Scott shared, "Energy was important, and we needed to work hard at keeping that energy up. We had to remind ourselves that if we didn't build a better product, people could die, and this project was about saving lives. A number of months into the project, right before the Easter holiday, morale was down. We'd been working 14-16-hour days, 6 days a week, and we all had to be reminded that our customers—the men and women in uniform—worked 24/7. I made a deal with my team: meet the weekly goals by Friday and not only would everyone get both Saturday and Sunday off to enjoy the holiday, I would also come into work on Monday dressed as the Easter bunny. My team followed through and on Monday morning, I kept my commitment, arriving at our weekly meeting dressed in a full Easter bunny costume that I had hunted down over the holiday weekend. I sat in my regular chair, where I'd normally be dressed in my business suit, kept our standard agenda, and ran the meeting like every previous Monday meeting. Everyone was laughing and smiling. It was a good time. More importantly, it re-energized the team and reconnected us with our purpose."

As I worked to renew my personal energy, I needed to reflect on my "kW," which included rediscovering what fueled me from deep within. In taking the time to reflect on *knowing why*, I reconnected with my own purpose: *To leave the world a better place than I found it, by bringing out the best in myself and others by being of service as a fun, energizing, caring leader.*

kW Power Up: Energizing Knowing Why

1. Take a moment to think about your personal and professional goals. Most of us start with asking what we want to achieve or who we want to become, yet very few of us take the time to ask why these goals are important to us. When setting a goal, take time to reflect and consider:

   - Why is this important to me?
   - Why do I want to achieve or accomplish this goal?
   - Why does it matter to me?
   - Why would this make a difference in my life?

2. Now ask yourself the following questions, taking the time to truly reflect on your answers.

- Is my *why* fueled with a burning desire?
- Does my *why* have the intensity to motivate me to do what it takes to reach my goal?
- Would anything stop me from reaching my goal? If so, why is what's stopping me more important than reaching my goal?
- What would I need to change to supercharge my *why* to make it an unstoppable driving force?

Powering Your Personal Energy

By igniting our "kW" and becoming crystal clear in *knowing who* we are, *knowing what* we want, and *knowing why* it's important to us, we transform into energized leaders. With incredible potential, our capacity to ignite our personal energy is only limited by how much we choose to limit ourselves. As energized leaders, we wisely choose how to fuel our personal energy, igniting our "kW" to fuel our full potential, and in doing so we energize others around us to do the same.

When it comes to personal energy, I find it helpful to think of the simple circuit. One in which we have an unlimited potential and capacity to positively power our lives. One in which we have the control to fuel our goals and dreams, simply by flipping a switch and energizing action. As with a circuit, we will encounter resistance, obstacles, and emotions that will challenge the flow as we drive toward our goals and more fulfilled lives. By fueling our "kW" and creating clarity in *knowing who* we are, *knowing what* we want, and *knowing why* we want it, we generate the ability to overcome resistance in our lives.

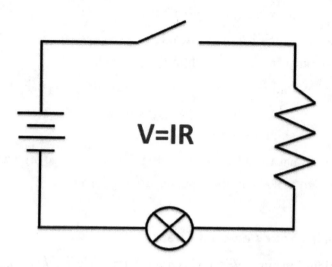

With a simple circuit, Ohm's Law (V=IR) reflects how voltage is directly proportional to the amount of electrical current flowing through a resistance. In powering our lives, think of V=IR in the following way: *The value "V" that "I" create is directly proportional to the responsibility "R" that I take for generating it.*

Our personal value is our self-worth, the value we bring to our relationships, and the value we provide in the services we offer to others and in our careers. By choosing to take responsibility for how we power our thoughts, behaviors, and actions, we put ourselves in charge of our lives. Furthermore, when we take responsibility for valuing ourselves, we increase our self-esteem, generating more self-confidence and powering our ability to provide greater value to others.

My friend Cybil Smith creatively defines our personal power as:

- P – our potential
  - O – the opportunities we pursue
    - W – the wisdom we carry
      - E – the effort we exert
        - R – the responsibility we take

I love how her definition captures that igniting our personal power is our responsibility! Energized leaders know taking responsibility for fueling their value will positively power their lives and the lives of those around them.

We can take the simple circuit analogy further, reframing the formula for power, or P=IV. In this case P=IV becomes: *My personal power "P" is directly proportional to how "I" take responsibility for generating value "V" in the world.*

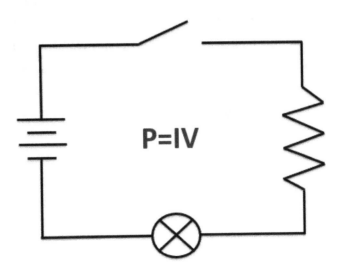

You can use P=IV, as I do, to energize your personal power by simply asking yourself on a regular basis: *"How can I power more value?"*

Variations of this question include yet are not limited to:

- How can I power more value as an individual?
- How can I power more value to this situation?
- How can I power more value to this relationship?
- How can I power more value to this project?
- How can I power more value to my organization?

"How can I power more value?" becomes the mantra of an energized leader. Making it a habit to continuously ask yourself how you can power more value will maximize your personal energy. By flipping our power switch and taking responsibility for our personal energy, we take charge of our lives. We tap into our incredible potential, energizing ourselves and our dreams. In charging toward our goals, we have the capacity to overcome any resistance we will encounter. We're happier, healthier, and more fulfilled in our personal lives. We power more productivity and profitability in our professional lives. By choosing to power more value, we become energized leaders.

While simple, when it comes to personal energy, V=IR and P=IV are extremely powerful and loaded formulas. Putting them into practice requires synthesizing all three "kWs."

Knowing who we are and being honest about our strengths and weaknesses—and how we need to grow takes courage. While *knowing what* we want may seem simple, taking action, measuring our progress, listening to feedback, being willing to learn, and adjust our strategies to ensure success takes commitment. Finally, we need powerful *whys* that continue to fuel our momentum, help us overcome frustration, and keep us from quitting and decreasing our value. Creating clarity in *knowing who* you are, *knowing what* you want, and *knowing why* you want it, isn't easy, and it takes work to power our personal energy.

Simply defined, energy is the capacity for work, and within each of us is a depth of energy that can be positively or negatively fueled. As energized leaders, we need to realize how much capacity is always there, and ultimately, the energy we power—positive or negative—will make or break our success. It is our responsibility to personally power the positive energy. As energized leaders, when we find ways to ignite our personal energy, our own "kW"—and the collective "kW" within our organizations—we create unstoppable forces to power unlimited creativity, growth and positive transformation.

Renewing my personal energy wasn't an easy task, but taking the time to recharge my "kW" and continuing to do so on an on-going basis has been worth it. It's been a number of years since I returned to the energy industry, and I continue to use the strategies presented in this chapter to power my personal energy. When I stepped into a role as a senior manager overseeing a large team that supported a portfolio of energy efficiency programs, I chose to be an energized leader and to help ignite the "kW" of our team. While I've moved on to new roles within the industry, I continue to receive feedback on the value I provided while serving in that role from team members and clients.

Returning to the energy industry has proven rewarding. I'm happier, more energized, and fulfilled in my life and career. Using V=IR, I've taken responsibility for the value I generate within my industry, and I energize P=IV, asking myself regularly "How can I power more value?" Remember how I wanted to make it an "inside job" energizing people and organizations with the energy industry? I'm doing just that by leading workshops on powering personal energy and energized leadership for energy companies and organizations!

While time is not a renewable resource, we can renew our personal energy. As energized leaders, when we wisely choose how to fuel our personal energy, ignite our "kW" and take responsibility for powering more value, we will positively energize ourselves and others around us to do the same. I believe our personal energy, our "kW," is our most powerful, renewable, "human energy" resource, and each day we get to choose how to energize it. As you step into your power and become an energized leader, how will you choose to focus your unlimited potential and energize the power of:

• *k*nowing *W*ho • *k*nowing *W*hat • *k*nowing *W*hy

Nathalie Osborn helps burned-out professionals fuel success, unplug stress, and energize their lives and careers. With a passion for inspiring efficiency, productivity, and teamwork, she empowers her clients with strategies she personally used to supercharge a highly accomplished 20-year energy industry career, where she implemented over $500M in energy efficiency, renewable energy, and sustainability programs. A Certified Canfield Success Principles Trainer and certified in many FranklinCovey content areas, she delivers highly interactive transformational masterclasses, workshops, and coaching solutions to renew and recharge your personal energy.

Nathalie continues to power value in the energy industry. She has served on the boards of multiple organizations, including the American Solar Energy Society (ASES), Advancing Women in Energy (AWE), and Michigan Energy Options (MEO). Nathalie is also a sought after speaker on Powering Personal Energy, Energized Leadership, and Positively Powering the Workplace. Learn more at www.nathalieosborn.com

CHAPTER 4

Your Greatest
Leadership Challenge
Develop the Courage to LEAD

by Neel Raman

Knowing yourself is the beginning of all wisdom.

~ ARISTOTLE

Leadership always evolves. This means the knowledge, skills, and competencies required to elevate your leadership performance will constantly change.

One thing that will not change, however, is the importance of leading yourself first before you lead others. This is your greatest leadership challenge.

The problem many leaders face today is they are expected to lead others effectively, even though they cannot lead themselves well.

What leaders need to do today is expanding. The table below outlines a few common leadership expectations and what's now required.

Common Leadership Expectations	New Leadership Requirements
Set and achieve business goals	Keep up with the speed of change and focus on continuous improvement
Focus on individual and team performance	Collaborate with other leaders to ensure workers find meaning in their roles
Manage risks	Create a safe space for all team members to thrive
Execute strategies to maintain operational efficiencies	Demonstrate authenticity and trust inner guidance for solutions

Table 1: Common Leadership Expectations versus New Leadership Requirements

While common leadership expectations will remain, how you lead needs to change. You will not meet the new leadership requirements and lead others effectively if you do not know how to lead yourself well first.

Just imagine how your leadership will improve if you can lead yourself well and have the courage to be your true self.

You are not a congruent or credible leader if you do not lead yourself first. And you cannot lead yourself if you do not know yourself.

If knowing yourself is the beginning of all wisdom, how do you find out who you are?

The premise of this chapter is leadership begins with you. When you focus on self-leadership, you will bring the best out of yourself and others.

Leaders Are Developed

It's a common misconception there are people who are natural-born leaders.

Anyone can become a powerful leader when they focus on their growth and learn more about who they are. This requires courage.

Early in my career, I learned the importance of knowing your true self if I wanted to become the best leader I could be. I had been in a production supervisor role for a manufacturing company. My responsibilities included improving machine run time and reducing material waste.

My manager had an engineering background and had a lot of technical knowledge and experience operating machines. He knew what to do to increase machine efficiencies and expected his supervisors to meet their production targets.

Machine breakdown was a common occurrence. Whenever a machine broke down and caused orders to be late, he would lose his temper. Since he had more knowledge about the machines than anyone else, often, he would fix them himself.

> *If we have a low level of self-awareness, we cannot lead others to become their best selves. It starts with self-leadership, which anyone can master.*

He was not pleasant to be around when he had to fix machines. He would curse and throw tools to express his anger. As a young supervisor, I remember thinking that was not a good way to cope with unplanned situations. I often stayed out of his way, just in case a tool ricocheted off a machine and hit me. He did not set the right leadership example.

Even though the company offered management and leadership training programs, they did not focus on how a person leads their life. That made me want to learn more about myself, so I could influence and inspire others to become their best selves. As I focused more on my personal development, it made me a better coach, trainer, and leader.

If we have a low level of self-awareness, we cannot lead others to become their best selves. It starts with self-leadership, which anyone can master. If we focus on self-leadership, we will know how to empower others to become the best leader they can be.

To influence others to reach new levels of performance and accelerate achievements, we must have a plan to focus on self-leadership.

Here's the plan to overcome your greatest leadership challenge:

1. Master the LEAD model.
2. Elevate your leadership confidence.
3. Become a leader worth following.

The LEAD model, as shown in the image below, is a simple, yet powerful tool you can use.

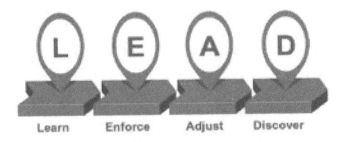

Figure 1: The LEAD Model

The LEAD model has four sections, which are Learn, Enforce, Adjust and Discover.

In the rest of this chapter, you will learn three practices for each section to improve your self-leadership, so that you can master the LEAD model, elevate your leadership confidence, and become a leader worth following.

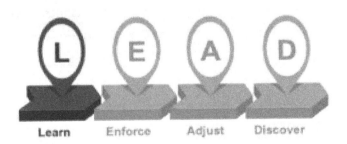

Figure 2: Learn

The goal is to gain self-awareness. Your results reflect your level of self-awareness.

Increasing your self-awareness is an ongoing practice, because things continuously evolve and change.

Here are three practices that will help you gain more self-awareness.

Practice 1: Listen to your inner voice

All great things begin from within. Relying on what you see, hear, smell, taste, and touch means you depend only on things externally. What goes on externally, the circumstances and situations, will always change.

If you only go by what's happening outside, you will always react. Leadership starts from within, which means leading from the inside out.

Actions you can take to listen to your inner voice include:

- Develop your intuition.
- Apply mindfulness techniques (which includes meditation, breathing exercises and releasing techniques).
- Build in quiet time each day for self-reflection.

When you do, you will:

- Make better, inspired decisions.
- Reduce mental clutter and overwhelm.
- Not second-guess if you are doing the right thing or not.

Practice 2: Leverage others for better outcomes

If you want to go fast, go alone. If you want to go far, go together.
~ African Proverb

It's highly probable someone has already done what you want to achieve. Instead of figuring everything out yourself, it's smart to take advantage of other people's knowledge and experience.

They can offer you support and help increase your confidence to achieve what you want.

Actions you can take to leverage others for better outcomes include:

- Identify the skills you want to improve or develop.
- Seek advice from others who already have those skills.
- Design a personal growth plan to develop those skills.

When you do, you will:

- Generate new ideas and opportunities.
- Progress faster to your goals.
- Form new partnerships.

Practice 3: Limit unproductive inputs

You receive information from the time you wake up to when you go to sleep. What you take in will affect your attitude, the results you produce, and how you lead yourself.

A simple way to focus on what's important is to limit your inputs. This means to pay attention only to what will get you closer to an outcome you want.

Actions you can take to limit unproductive inputs include:

- Eliminate distractions, interruptions, and noise.
- Avoid non-essential negative news or conversations.
- Study or follow a few mentors to go further, faster.

When you do, you will:

- Have more clarity.
- Replace unproductive habits with productive ones.
- Improve your ability to focus.

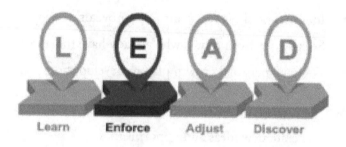

Figure 3: Enforce

The goal is to apply what you learn. Learning for the sake of it is not helpful. Knowledge is not power. It is potential power.

Having knowledge will only make a difference if you put it to use.

When you enforce what you learn, you will build self-trust, which means you will learn faster.

Here are three practices that will help you apply what you learn.

Practice 1: Enhance your motivation

Your level of motivation will affect what you do or don't. If you have a high level of motivation, you will focus better and give more energy to what you want to do.

Everyone occasionally experiences a dip in motivation. The good news is, you can generate motivation and direct it to the outcomes you want.

There are things you can do daily to enhance your motivation, which will help you apply what you learn.

Actions you can take to enhance your motivation include:

- Have a purpose or intention for everything you do.
- Develop habits that will keep you motivated longer.
- Create supportive environments.

When you do, you will:

- Use your time better.
- Produce better outcomes.
- Feel better about yourself and what you are doing.

Practice 2: Educate others to lock in what you learn

When you share what you learn with others, you will understand it better. If you want to develop the courage to lead effectively, teach others.

A mindset that will help is, "We teach what we need to learn the most."

If you want to make a bigger impact, place more importance on the difference you can make in other people's lives, instead on your fears and self-doubt.

Actions you can take to educate others to lock in what you learn include:

- Ask questions to find out what they want.
- Share mistakes you have made and what you learned from them.
- Provide support and encouragement to reinforce key lessons.

When you do, you will:

- Improve your communication skills.
- Have more influence with those you lead.
- Increase your self-confidence.

Practice 3: Elevate your performance and achievements

You, like everyone, want to perform better and achieve more success. When you increase your performance and achievements, your leadership influence will rise, which will also help bring out the best in others.

There are many strategies and techniques you can apply to raise your performance and achievements. Not everything applies or is relevant to everyone. A smarter option is to focus on fewer things that will have the most impact.

Actions you can take to elevate your performance and achievements include:

- Create an achievement or productivity system that works for you.
- Evaluate your performance and what you produce daily.
- Hold yourself accountable.

When you do, you will:

- Give more attention to your priorities.
- Stretch and grow as a person.
- Generate more positive emotions.

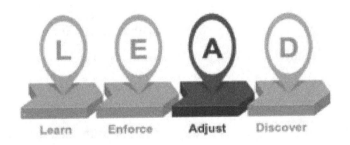

Figure 4: Adjust

The goal is to review what is and isn't working. Your objective is to continue to do more of what is working and change what isn't.

If you want to advance your self-leadership, face what's not working head-on and adjust your approach so you can achieve your objectives.

Here are three practices that will help you review what is and isn't working, so you can make the adjustments needed to reach your goals.

Practice 1: Ask for feedback

Feedback is often referred to as "the breakfast of champions," because those who have a growth mindset always look for ways to improve.

Receiving timely and useful feedback is a powerful motivator. The key is to remain open to all feedback.

Not all feedback is useful. If you develop the habit of asking for regular feedback, you will know what's useful and what's not.

Actions you can take to ask for feedback include:
- Schedule regular check-in sessions with a coach, mentor, or manager.
- Make giving and receiving feedback a normal practice.
- Define your goals of feedback and ensure they are relevant to something you want to achieve.

When you do, you will:
- Receive new ideas for improvement.
- Respond quicker to what's not working well.
- Make better informed decisions.

Practice 2: Align your actions to your big picture

The big picture is where you are going or what you want to achieve. It is your end result. It is what matters most and what you are working to accomplish.

To stay focused on the big picture requires clarity and a commitment to stay on course. That will help you align your actions to your outcomes.

Actions you can take to align to your big picture include:

- Define your most important goals and link your weekly and daily activities to them.
- Focus on what you do best, your core competencies, and delegate the rest.
- Keep your goals front-of-mind and know why you want to achieve them.

When you do, you will:

- Eliminate unnecessary activities, which will speed your progress.
- Place greater importance on what you do daily and why it matters.
- Manage your energy and effort a lot better.

Practice 3: Adapt to change

Change is a part of life. Things continually evolve. This means you must learn to adapt, so you can deal with change better.

Most times, going through change is not difficult. The real challenge is what you tell yourself about any change you experience.

You can deal with change better if you manage your emotions well and let go of how you want it to happen.

Actions you can take to adapt to change include:

- Form a mental picture or vision of what is possible.
- Identify obstacles you may face and develop strategies to overcome them.
- Ask for help if you struggle to cope.

When you do, you will:

- Improve your mental and emotional well-being.
- Learn to embrace change rather than resist it.
- Attract opportunities that can inspire new goals.

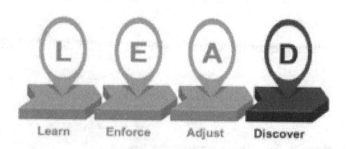

Figure 5: Discover

The goal is to uncover new possibilities. As you learn, enforce and adjust, your leadership style will emerge.

If you stay open to what emerges, you will discover your unique leadership style, which can help make you a better, authentic leader.

Practice 1: Define your new identity

How you view yourself becomes your identity. It is your self-image.

To define a new identity will require you to improve your self-image. To develop the courage to lead well will require you to improve your self-image.

Your self-image will affect your confidence and how you relate to others. You will never outperform your self-image.

This means to become a better leader and achieve new results, you have to shift your identity and develop a better self-image. This will require you to take a stand for who you want to become and stay committed to it.

Actions you can take to define your new identity include:

- Change your self-talk to focus on your positive qualities and who you are becoming.
- Stop comparing yourself to others.
- Acknowledge and celebrate your wins.

When you do, you will:

- Broaden your perspective and change how you view your leadership abilities.
- Have the courage to take risks to achieve what you want.
- Gain new self-belief.

Practice 2: Develop the right systems and processes

Systems and processes make it easier to stay on track and continue to progress to your goals.

A challenge you will face is to stay focused on what matters most. If you don't have the right systems and processes, you will waste time, energy and resources on things that are not important.

Systems and processes will help identify what you need to give attention to and when.

Actions you can take to develop the right systems and processes include:

- Identify the activities you do currently.
- Categorize those activities according to your priorities.
- Find ways to continually improve.

When you do, you will:

- Not lose sight of your vision or big picture.
- Respond faster to setbacks or failures, which means you will adapt quicker.
- Avoid decision fatigue, which means you will have greater clarity of thought.

Practice 3: Discipline yourself to stay on course

Discipline is the ability to give yourself a command and stick to it. Learning to discipline yourself will make a big difference in how you think, feel, and act, and will also help you stay on course.

To stay disciplined will require the use of your will, which is a mental faculty you have. The smart way to use your will is to make a conscious choice to stay focused on your goals, no matter what is going on.

Using your will means holding the image of what you want and who you want to become in your mind, and acting in alignment with that image.

Actions you can take to discipline yourself to stay on course include:

- Avoid multitasking and focus on one thing at a time.
- Use reward or consequence as a motivator to stay focused.
- Know your triggers and patterns, so you can remove distractions and temptations.

When you do, you will:

- Solve your problems a lot faster.
- Have a higher level of self-trust.
- Increase your self-awareness and become a better leader.

When you apply the practices in the LEAD model, you will not question whether you can lead effectively, because how you lead yourself will transfer to how you lead others.

Always remember, you cannot lead others effectively if you cannot lead yourself well first. As your leadership evolves, those you lead will also raise their performance and increase what they produce.

Your greatest leadership challenge is to develop the courage to LEAD, which is to learn, enforce, adjust, and discover. When you do, you will know how to lead yourself well, which will also improve how you lead others.

Best of luck as you become the best leader you can be.

Reflection

1. My biggest takeaway from this chapter was...

_____

_____

_____

_____

_____

2. The practice that will bring me the greatest benefit is...

_____

_____

_____

_____

_____

3. The actions I will take after reading this chapter are…

_____

_____

_____

_____

_____

Your FREE Gift

To take your learnings further, I'd like to offer you a summary of all the practices, with additional resources that will make it easier to apply what you have learned.

To access your free gift, go to: https://neelraman.com/lead

Neel Raman is a #1 international best-selling author whose books include *Ignite Your Leadership*, *Building High-Performing Teams*, *Transition from Manager to Coach*, *Sustaining a Leadership Culture*, and *Hoops and Freedom*.

As a certified coach and an authority on the topics of personal development, high performance, personal leadership and business improvement, Neel has helped leaders, business owners and organisations increase performance, productivity and profits.

Neel has spoken at a TEDx event in India and has trained with some of the best trainers and speakers in the world including Jack Canfield, the co-creator of the *Chicken Soup for the Soul* book series and author of *The Success Principles*.

Neel is a certified Canfield Trainer in *The Success Principles* and *The Canfield Methodology* and can assist businesses and individuals who want to achieve greater success through different experiential training programs, online courses and coaching programs.

To find more out more about Neel, visit NeelRaman.com

CHAPTER 5

Intentional Possibility
The Magic of Happiness and the Power of Change

by Sergio Sedas, PhD

Manage people and people will get things done. Lead them and they will be inspired into action. Enroll them into possibility and they will change the world.

— SERGIO SEDAS, PHD

The room was full of people when William "Red" Whittaker suddenly stood up and declared, "Within a year, we will have designed, built, and deployed the first robot in history to enter a live volcano in Antarctica."

Those words marked the beginning of DANTE, the first robot in history developed by Carnegie Mellon University to enter a live volcano in Antarctica. Within a year, a group of young graduate students led by Red, raised over two and a quarter million dollars, united NASA, Carnegie Mellon University, the University of New Mexico, the United Nations, and other organizations, and fully empowered a team of forty students and staff that designed, built, and deployed DANTE into a live volcano in the freezing grasps of Mount Erebus.

In 1993, a year after Red stood up and made his declaration, CNN covered the deployment of DANTE. Within a year, we made this declaration of possibility possible.

I was one of the forty graduate students that participated in the development of DANTE. I clearly remember that day when Red said those words. I was drawn into them not as a vision, not as an idea, but as something that already was.

In everyone's mind, DANTE—and the possibility of DANTE—was real. So real, in fact, that NASA donated over two million dollars and contributed time on a newly developed high-speed satellite communication system to remotely operate the robot. So real, that we woke up every day engaged in this new possibility creating, designing, working, asking, and doing. So real, that every day we woke up eagerly looking for, identifying, and overcoming challenges of the unknown.

You see, the moment Red made his declaration, the possibility of DANTE became real. It was not a vision. It was not a project. It was not an idea. In his mind, and in our minds, it simply was. We lived our lives in the reality of DANTE, creating and engaging, until DANTE crystalized and took form.

That is the power of possibility. Tap into this power, and you can move your organization into new, incredible heights.

Possibility goes beyond vision ~ it carries purpose and passion

On September 12, 1962, at Rice University, John F. Kennedy rose up and declared that within a decade we would have a man on the moon. With that speech, he united the world in a common mission. Before that instant, people were going about their own business, but the moment he made that speech, everything changed.

People began to live the possibility as if it were true. Scientists began to look for and solve the challenges that we would have to overcome. Congress began to look for the money to fund the project. Schools all around the world began to teach their students about it, and on July 20, 1969, millions of people were glued to the TV, following the event, and waiting for Neil Armstrong to take his first memorable step on the moon.

Putting a man on the moon is not the only place that possibility happens. It happens all around you. Possibility created the building you are sitting in. It created parks, schools, summer concerts in the park, and millions of volunteer programs around the world. Many people have tapped into the power of possibility and caused things to happen. Behind everything that touches our lives is the power of possibility. It even caused this book to exist and end up in your hands.

The possibility of *creating a world without poverty*, declared by Professor of Economics Muhammad Yanus, developed the concept of loans awarded to entrepreneurs too poor to qualify for traditional bank loans. In 2006, Professor Yanus was awarded the Nobel Peace

Prize for "his efforts through microcredit to create economic and social development from below."

Rosa Ramirez created ADANEC, a network of doctors, nurses, hospitals, and donors that provides free healthcare to children with congenital heart diseases. YouTube, Vimeo, Flickr, and other web platforms created the possibility for everyone to share and communicate through photo and video. Skype, WhatsApp, and other communication platforms created the possibility for people to communicate freely around the world.

Just like those above, the possibilities of *prosperity for everyone, a strong creative environment, people openly expressing their views,* or *education for everyone,* could be among the driving forces behind many new initiatives in your company.

Possibility is a powerful driving force

When people are living in possibility, they are driven. They have a sense of direction and are motivated and inspired into action. They create. They face adversity and creatively find alternatives to overcome their challenges. They communicate and ask for what they need. If one of their projects fails, they simply stand up, learn from the experience, move forward, and try again.

Give people a powerful possibility—one which they resonate with—and you will have created a powerful driving force. Recreate the message of possibility, let them be creative, and then set them free. They will expand your possibility and give it a life of its own. In the process, they will create projects, programs, and initiatives that live within this possibility. They will plan. They will manage.

They will execute. They will pour their hearts into these initiatives as these initiatives become their own.

You have the power of intentionally creating possibility

You have the power to intentionally create possibility. When you do, you will inspire people to take action and give life to projects and initiatives that make wonderful things happen.

Everyone can; and without knowing, almost everyone has.

Let me give you a common, everyday simple example. Have you ever thrown a party? You think about it. You set a date. You talk to friends about it. As you describe the party, in your mind you begin to create a clear image of what it is and how it will take place. You imagine the people that are walking through the door. You imagine hearing some of their conversations. You imagine what you will wear and what you will eat. You create this movie that is running consciously inside your head.

You suddenly live your life as if the party is real. Then you take actions that are consistent with the possibility of the party. You confirm the date, talk to people, inquire about catering, and you make your list. In your mind, the party is no longer an idea; the party simply is. It has become real. And this reality begins to drive you.

Possibility is contagious. When you talk to other people

> *Give people a powerful possibility—one which they resonate with—and you will have created a powerful driving force.*

about the party, they begin to compose their own movies. They imagine the people, the conversations, the food, and the layout. In their minds, the party is no longer an idea, it simply *is*. It has become their new reality. They enroll in the conversation; they go from being passive listeners to active participants. They talk about it. They Tweet about it. They post on Facebook. They communicate. "What are you going to wear?" "Can I ride with you?" "Are you taking someone?"

The people invited take an active role in the organization and execution of the party. They invite people. They raise funds. They cooperate. They find the place. They bring the food. Your party is now their party.

When this happens, the party becomes alive and carries a life of its own. It no longer matters if you make it to the party. The party will happen. Someone will bring live music. Someone will bring stage lights. People are engaged, and a simple idea that you created has united many people into action.

OHANA

A number of years ago, two young high school students decided to run a fundraising campaign around the Christmas holiday to raise funds to buy jackets and donate them to people who lived in isolated, low-income communities in Mexico. The campaign was a success, and soon after, they delivered the jackets.

However, while the students were enjoying the comfort of a warm holiday at home, they came to realize that while they were sitting comfortably in their homes, the people, who benefited from their earlier efforts, were suffering from cold, hunger, and immense challenges every day. While they brought temporary comfort to their beneficiaries' lives, nothing really changed. The students wanted to do more.

They took it upon themselves to create the possibility of a program that would forever change the mindset and reality of people in need. Within this possibility, they decided to create a one-week summer camp for orphans who were cared for by the state. These kids were mostly abandoned or rescued from difficult homes.

The students shared this new possibility with their parents, the school principal, the teachers, and other students. Pretty soon, people submerged into this possibility. The principal lent them the gym, teachers and students formed committees. They raised funds, approached orphanages, and they designed a program. They ran their first event.

Last summer, I was walking by the Student Center at my university, Tecnológico de Monterrey, when I heard a lot of laughter. I was drawn into it and saw a large group of students and children. I went over and asked what it was all about. OHANA was hosting one of their summer camps, and over 100 volunteers were participating. There were children between the ages of 6 and 12 organized into groups. Each group inspired specific values and had a set of activities to help children grow, gain self-confidence, dream, and see themselves in a bright and positive future.

OHANA had grown. In just a few years, students inspired by this possibility, took it upon themselves to create additional chapters in their schools. At the time of this publication, over four chapters exist and have multiplied across high schools and colleges.

The founders have long since graduated college, yet OHANA has a life of its own.

Learn to intentionally create possibility

Learn to intentionally use the power of possibility to inspire your entire organization and the people you serve to new heights. In my book series, *Intentional Possibility* and *Intentional Possibility in Action*, I outline an elaborate study of possibility and detail the steps you can follow to intentionally create possibility within your organization. In these two volumes, I help you develop new skills by inventing possibility and developing and creating a project that moves over 200 people.

The six steps that form the base of creating possibility are as follows:

Find your purpose and declare a possibility. Declare something in possibility that moves your organization; a reason to be that is powerful, engaging, inspiring, and above all, something that will transcend time, place, and you.

Enroll others. Possibility grows in the minds of people. Share possibility. Enroll people into it. Help them resonate and make it their own. Invite them to enlist and contribute, to communicate and celebrate, and to be a part of the possibility. Invite them to enjoy. Form your team, attract volunteers, and attract time and resources.

Define a project, event, program, or initiative that lives within this possibility. Possibility manifests itself in every project, event, program, and initiative that we develop. So, once possibility is clear, allow your team to brainstorm and come up with projects that you can develop. Let the project impact and involve a large volume of people. Plan it. Organize it. Then be ready to set it free.

Lay out a plan. Once you have a clear idea of what you want to do, you need to create a plan. Define activities, resources, and people you need to get the plan done. Identify a leader who will oversee the project and additional leaders who will oversee the development of the plan. However, remember that the purpose is not the project—it is not the plan—it is the possibility that you have created.

Keep this in mind as you give your project the freedom to grow and adapt itself to fulfill its purpose.

Get into action. Communicate clearly. Prepare your team. Encourage them, and above all, act. Action will create the momentum you need to see your possibility happen. Help everyone stay focused and establish the networks, accountability partnerships, and methods to get things done.

Acknowledge and celebrate. Possibility starts out in your mind. It manifests itself through language and actions. Take the time to be present in every communication, action, and success. Constantly acknowledge and celebrate with your team.

Learn to overcome the showstoppers

In the process of creating possibility and making great projects, events, and initiatives happen, you will find yourself facing five of the most common roadblocks that will attempt to hold you back. They are:

- Lack of clarity
- Resistance
- Ego
- Expectations
- Fear

As reviewed in our book, there are ways to defeat these roadblocks. Some of the things you can do to overcome these forces are to be extremely clear about what you want to accomplish, move into action, and let go.

Learn to Go Pro

Once you learn how to create possibility, and through it, ignite the spark on projects and initiatives, you must train for the best. Go Pro. Learn the skills you need to inspire, and lead your team into creating an amazing possibility that takes a life of its own.

Learn how to awaken drive and passion. Learn how to communicate, how to inspire, and how to enroll. Learn how to help your team members grow by teaching them how to communicate and lead. Learn how to help your team stay motivated and focused. Learn how to live with integrity, and use it to balance your life and attract the people you need to bring in the resources and time to make things happen.

What do you do?

A few weeks ago, I walked into a postal station. I asked the clerk, "What do you do?"

"I sort mail," he said.

"What for?"

"To organize it and have it ready for our customers," he replied.

"And then what?"

"When they come in, I give it to them."

"And then what? What do your customers do?" I prodded him further.

"They open up their packages." He seemed puzzled that I was asking so many questions.

"And then what?"

"Well, many leave happy, because they received something that they were waiting for."

"Ok, so sorting mail and packages allows people to receive their packages and be happy because of it. So, would it be fair to say that you bring happiness to your customers by helping them receive things that they want and need?"

"Yes!" His face lit up, like he just discovered something.

"Ok, so now think about your business. What else could you do to bring happiness to your customers by helping them receive things that they want and need?" I continued my inquiry.

"Hmmm, I could have a corkboard on which customers can post things that they do not need anymore. I could have a computer on-site, which would allow people to order anything they wanted online to be delivered at our facility. I could have special discounts and programs that would help them save money. I could find out what people buy the most and contact suppliers for a discount. I could open up a store and offer some of these things they need more of. I could home deliver their things and save them the trouble of coming to us. I could..." He was beginning to see the possibilities of expanding his services, and likely for the first time.

By changing what he did from the action of sorting mail to the possibility of making people happy by helping them receive the things that they want and need, he was able to come up with many creative ideas, projects, and initiatives to make it happen. Furthermore, thinking about the possibility of helping people motivated him.

How can you define your business? What do you do? Who do you help? How do you help them? What positive value do you bring to the people you serve? To your team? To your suppliers?

What statement of possibility can you declare that inspires you and your organization to create new programs, initiatives, projects, and ventures?

How can you express what you do so that you are inspired, moved, and driven? From this reflection, define a statement of possibility. Write it down:

_____

_____

_____

Possibility in your workplace and your community

You can also create a statement of possibility that impacts your workplace and your community. Think about your ideal workplace and your relationship with your community. What does it look like? How do people interact? How do people communicate? How do they grow? What inspires them? What moves them? Is there a place to be creative and express and share your ideas? Do people have time to be with their family? Does everyone feel significant? Do people contribute to each other? Do people know each other? Do they share moments together?

Define a statement of possibility, and write it down.

_____

_____

_____

Create a project, event, program, or initiative

Now that you have written a statement of possibility, take the time to come up with projects, events, programs, and initiatives that you could create to manifest that possibility. Coming from a space of possibility, ask yourself:

- What can you do for your customers?
- What new products could you develop?
- What can you do for your team?
- How can you create an outstanding working environment?
- Can you think of new ways of doing things?
- How can you involve the community?
- Can you form new partnerships?
- Can you think of new and interesting giveaways?
- What about new ways to serve?

Just let your mind go free, and create within the space of possibility.

Make it happen

Now that you have defined possibility, and you have brainstormed a number of projects, events, programs, and initiatives, it is time to make them happen.

Pick one of these projects and describe it, in as much detail as you can. A great level of detail will give clarity to your project.

Start making a plan. Make a list of all of the things that need to get done in order for your project to happen. Think about estimating the budget, getting the money, inviting the people, forming your team, and all of the things that must get done.

Enroll others into the possibility. Enlist people onto your team, and find people that resonate with what you want to do. You are looking for people that are willing to jump in and take it on as if it were their own.

Communicate frequently, and monitor your success. Remember daily to keep the possibility you are creating alive.

One final note

You have the power to intentionally create a wonderful, prosperous, and significant world for your family, your customers, your organization, and your community.

Just remember, declare powerful possibility, enroll others, and together you will change the world.

Dr. Sergio Sedas is CEO of Solution Center Group and professor at the EGADE Business School at Tecnológico de Monterrey.

He is former head of the mechatronics undergraduate program at Tecnológico de Monterrey and founder of multiple hi-tech companies. He has a PhD in Robotics and Computational Design from Carnegie Mellon University. For over 25 years he has developed innovative industrial robotic and vision systems for Fortune 100 and Fortune 500 companies.

Interested in innovating leadership and education, in 2010 he began to research the human brain and human behavior to determine how to improve engagement, enhance intrinsic motivation, spark creativity and drive, increase resiliency and develop a strong sense of purpose. This led him to research the fields of neuroscience, positive psychology and cognitive psychology.

He is best-selling author of *Intentional Possibility: The Magic of Happiness and the Power of Change* and award-winning author of

Context Based Learning: Learning through Understanding and of a national program to develop resiliency, self-confidence, intrinsic motivation and a sense of purpose in young adults. He is also a founder of Solution Center Group, a company that helps people, companies, and organizations to live with passion and intentionally create possibilities.

His ideas have been presented at TEDx in India, U.S. Chamber of Commerce, Fortune 100 companies, and multiple international academic and industrial forums.

His website is: www.sergiosedas.com

Section Two
Leading Others

CHAPTER 6

Teams that Shine
Creating Conditions for Maximum Engagement

by Sally Dooley

None of us is as smart as all of us.
–Kenneth H. Blanchard, Author

The current turbulent global economy combined with skills shortage, talent wars, and transitioning into the Digital Age creates a real need for organisations to develop a sustainable competitive advantage through maximising the performance of their teams. In my work as a facilitator and executive coach, I repeatedly hear a genuine desire from leaders to create the kind of environment where their staff can really thrive. Sadly, I hear just as often, "But I don't have time!" or "I don't know how." This chapter highlights the huge costs of not investing time in what should be your most powerful asset—a highly engaged team—and outlines how to create the conditions for your team to shine and productivity to soar.

Have you ever worked with a truly dreadful team? I have, and it was one of the lowest times of my career, if not my life! This team was fragmented and lacked collaboration and purpose. In fact, it wasn't so much a team as a collection of individuals paid by the same employer.

When I reflect on the dysfunction of that team, the glaringly obvious stand-out was that most of us were functioning as square pegs in round holes. I was in a largely administrative role, which considering my distaste for detail and lack of organisational skills, was never going to work. I hungered for people contact and to work with someone I could encourage or connect with. Unfortunately, someone else occupied that role. I recall the frustration I felt and that team members were too disempowered to talk about what was really going on. My attempts to draw attention to the rather large elephant in the room backfired and cost me dearly. Eventually, I resigned.

Sadly, too many people have shared my experience, or something similar. They have found themselves in teams that had the potential to fly, but instead floundered along, eventually losing gifted people or watching as team members began to disengage.

So, why is engagement so important and disengagement such a concern? Well, one compelling reason is that disengaged staff have a huge impact on the bottom line. Recent research, the 2017 State of the Global Workforce, conducted by Gallup found that only a staggeringly low fifteen percent of employees in the one hundred and forty-two countries studied were actually engaged in their work. According to Gallup, a staff member is engaged if they are "emotionally invested in and focused on creating value for their organisations every day." The cost of this is significant. Gallup estimates that per year, actively disengaged staff drain somewhere in the vicinity of $450 to $550 billion (yes, that is billion) from U.S. organisations alone.

In another major research study noted in *Happiness at Work: Maximizing Your Psychological Capital for Success*, Jessica Pryce-Jones found that those who were happiest at work only take one and a half days off sick per year, compared with the average in the U.K. and U.S. of six days. In the public sector, it is even higher, ranging from eleven to twenty days. Imagine the accumulated cost of all that lost time!

> *What if we, as leaders, could create teams where roles and tasks are aligned with what people are best at and most passionate about, where people felt valued, and that their work was truly meaningful?*

Pryce's research also highlights that few people think they are utilising their full potential. This means, "organisations are not taking advantage of the huge amount of talent, goodwill, and energy which lie at their disposal. There is a massive resource at hand which, with a little effort, could easily be developed for everyone's benefit." In addition, when people feel engaged and productive at work, there are positive effects outside work as well. These lucky people experience higher levels of general life enjoyment and more frequently experience positive emotional states on a daily basis. The multiplier effect of engaged workers has the power to significantly influence families, communities, and life as we know it.

It seems clear: having engaged employees is not just about creating happy workplaces and happier workers: it is a bottom-line issue. It seems equally clear that the potential to create highly engaged teams exists, but is rarely harnessed. If the organisations and teams we lead are going to have any hope of thriving in the current context, we need to ensure they have fully engaged people.

What if we, as leaders, could create teams where roles and tasks are aligned with what people are best at and most passionate about, where people felt valued, and that their work was truly meaningful? Surely team members would be happier, more engaged, and ultimately, much more productive? From a wealth of research, the overwhelming findings are that we can create teams like that. It just takes an understanding of what the key drivers are for creating engagement, an honest appraisal of where your team sits now, and a strategic approach to transition forward.

Drivers for Greater Engagement

In considering the research and my experience of working with hundreds of leaders and team members, the strongest drivers I see for creating engaged teams are depicted in the framework below. Each driver will be considered in detail, with some practical suggestions for you to consider building into your leadership practice.

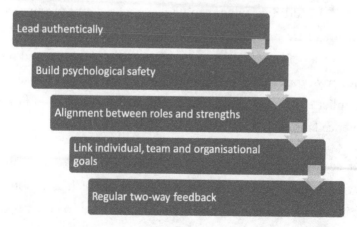

Lead authentically

If you want to become a great leader, gain the capacity to connect with your colleagues and customers at a deep level... or lower your aim.

—SUSAN SCOTT, AUTHOR OF *FIERCE LEADERSHIP*

Leadership begins with who you really are and your willingness to really connect with others in a genuine way. Leaders of teams that shine have mastered the art of authenticity, which is about being comfortable with who you are and courageous enough to let that guide the decisions you make, the way you behave, and how you interact with others. This capability is critical as it underpins the other engagement drivers.

Researchers Avolio, Luthans, and Walumbwa identify authentic leaders as sharing a number of characteristics including:

- awareness of how they think and behave;
- being perceived by others as aware of their own and others' valuable knowledge and strengths;
- awareness of their context, and;
- being confident, hopeful, optimistic, resilient, and of high moral character.

It seems that in today's context we want a little more from our leaders than just being good decision-makers, technically proficient, and knowing who and how to schmooze. To navigate their teams through the storms of downsizing, up-skilling, resource slashing, artificial intelligence, and escalating customer expectations, we need leaders who are in tune with themselves, have the capacity to connect with and strengthen others, and have a high level of integrity.

Their research also shows that there is a positive connection between a leader's capacity to lead authentically and the level of trust in their team. This means that leaders with high levels of self and other awareness, who are confident, optimistic, and resilient, create teams that have high levels of trust. These are the teams that shine!

What can you do?

So, how do you become an authentic leader able to build teams with a solid foundation of trust? Well, the answer to that could fill a hundred books, so I will narrow it down to one practice: the practice of real conversation. As Susan Scott, author of *Fierce Leadership: A Bold Alternative to the Worst "Best" Practices of Business Today*, so aptly expresses, "Our careers, our companies, our personal relationships, and our very lives succeed or fail, gradually then suddenly—one conversation at a time."

Our conversations matter, and for the human connection to be truly powerful it has to engage the heart as well as the mind. To lead more authentically means intentionally improving the quality of your conversations.

Over the next few weeks, set aside time daily to reflect on your conversations. Use these questions to notice what went well and what could have worked better:

- Were you really present, or was your mind elsewhere?

- Did you take the time to hear their perspective, or did you stay focused on yours?
- Did you share what you felt, or just what you thought?
- Did you hold back because of fear of what might eventuate if you said what you really wanted to?
- Did you consider how the other person might be interpreting your words and what impact they were having on them?
- Were you willing to have your positions and beliefs challenged?

How did you rate? Where do you most need to improve? Identify what specifically you want to do differently, and practice doing it.

Build Psychological Safety

A few years ago, Google undertook a massive study of its organisation to discover what made teams successful. They looked at every dimension imaginable, from the personality of the leader to how often the team socialised together outside of work. What they found surprised everyone! It turns out that where teams had a high level of psychological safety, the creative juices really flowed.

So, what is this psychological safety? In her book, *The Fearless Organization: Creating Psychological Safety in the Workplace for Learning, Innovation, and Growth*, Amy Edmonson notes that it boils down to a culture where each team member feels they are able to give voice to their ideas without fear of put-downs or punishments. In other words, psychological safety exists where there is a high level of trust across a group and a sense that its members have positive intent toward each other. This creates a culture where people feel safe enough to put themselves and their ideas out there.

Think about the cost of fear in organisations. It is fear that stops us from speaking up, from offering a new or untested idea, from reporting mistakes and from challenging the thinking of someone higher up the food chain than we are. Fear keeps us focused on watching our backs rather than on delivering the best results for our clients and stakeholders. While fear is the enemy of creativity and innovation, psychological safety is about minimising the fear that people experience at work so they can show up as their best selves.

As digital technology increasingly changes the nature of our work, the new essential capabilities are creativity, adaptability and collaboration. These thrive in a culture with a high level of psychological safety and lie stagnant where it is low or absent.

What can you do?

No matter what the culture of your team is right now, you can take steps to build a sense of psychological safety. Understand that it is a process and takes place over time as trust is established across the team. Here are some practical ways to get started:

- **Reframe failure** – To try something new or make a suggestion is risky business. People fear that they will get it wrong or look silly or fail to measure up in some way. The role of a leader is to be clear about the non-negotiables, and then explicitly and frequently communicate that the only failure is not being willing to try. When mistakes are made, conversations should be solution focused and encourage reflection and sharing of lessons learned.

- **Expect participation** – I once consulted with an engineering firm, and the CEO was frustrated with his team as they wouldn't ever offer ideas or suggestions. I attended a meeting he was leading with his team to observe him in action, and within minutes the reason for their non-participation was apparent! He was the first to speak on every topic, offering strong opinions and dismissing others' thoughts. It was obvious that everyone had just given up trying to influence him! I encouraged him to approach the meetings with curiosity, swapping open-ended questions for opinions, and allowing space for everyone to contribute. This could be something you try as well. It's also good to let the team know that you want to encourage more participation from each team member and that you value their input. Make it clear that team meetings are no longer a spectator sport! Acknowledge contributions and have one-on-one conversations with those who are reluctant to speak up to find out how you can support them to contribute.

- **Nurture team relationships** – You can fast track the level of psychological safety in your team by investing in strengthening team cohesion. There are many ways to do this, from team lunches to outdoor activities. One of the most frequent ways I work with teams is to use a tool that promotes self and other awareness in the team. For example, the Herrmann Brain Dominance Indicator© (HBDI) measures thinking preferences and offers many valuable insights including your communication, decision making, problem solving, and workplace relationship preferences. This promotes understanding of the diversity within the team and how it can be harnessed for more effective performance. It is also a fun process, and being willing to laugh together requires vulnerability, which is the foundation for trust.

Align roles and strengths

Identify a person's strengths. Define outcomes that play to those strengths. Find a way to count, rate or rank those outcomes. And then let the person run.

–MARCUS BUCKINGHAM, CO-AUTHOR, *FIRST BREAK ALL THE RULES*

When authors Buckingham and Coffman released their book, *First Break All the Rules: What the World's Greatest Managers Do Differently*, there were a few surprising recommendations. However, as they were based on the findings from Gallup's most extensive study involving over 80,000 managers in over 400 companies, the concepts rapidly gained momentum. One of the key findings was that the world's greatest managers don't focus on trying to fix their team members' weaknesses; rather they focused on building their strengths.

As reported in Gallup's 2017 State of the Global Workforce survey, when team members have the opportunity to work regularly in their areas of strength, they are much more likely to be highly engaged and productive. Practically, this means ensuring there is a strong alignment between what employees are naturally good at and the requirements of their job, or as Buckingham and Coffman expressed it, ensuring employees "have the opportunity to do what they do best every day." So, what are the benefits to focusing on strengths?

- **When our work is aligned with our strengths, we are more likely to enjoy it and want to invest more in building our expertise.** I think back to my undergraduate days, when I embarked on an accounting degree. As you already know, detail is not my thing, although I could have persevered and obtained my degree, I know I would never have excelled, because it would have just taken too much effort. In contrast, when I studied for my Masters in Training and Development, I excelled. Yes, it took long hours of focus, but it is so much easier to focus on something that you are passionate about rather than something that barely keeps you awake. We can exercise great discipline and become skillful in areas where we are not gifted, but developing a high level of expertise is most likely when we build on our strengths.

- **We feel more confident as we are more likely to be successful in an area of strength.** Self-confidence is powerful, but what do we really mean by it? In *Psychological Capital: Developing the Human Competitive Edge*, Fred Luthans, Carolyn M. Youssef, and Bruce Avolio, define it as "an individual's conviction (or confidence) about his or her abilities to mobilize the motivation, cognitive resources, and course of action needed to successfully execute a specific task within a given context." In terms of accounting, I struggled with all three aspects of that definition: I was not motivated (understatement!), doubted my cognitive capacity when it came to numbers, and was uncertain about how to execute any specific tasks. Conversely, in my chosen field of people development, I am passionate, intellectually engaged, and confident in my capacity to deliver great outcomes for my clients. As a result, I've experienced success, and as we know, success breeds success. With each success my confidence has grown.

Luthans and colleagues also note that, "Self-efficacious people are distinguished by five important characteristics: they set high goals for themselves and self-select into difficult tasks; they welcome and thrive on challenge; they are highly self-motivated; they invest the necessary effort to accomplish their goals; and when faced with obstacles, they persevere." Isn't this exactly what we want for our team members, as well as for ourselves? Focusing on strengths is the pathway to get us there.

So, how do we identify those strengths? I have seen in my own life and those with whom I have worked, that it is not always an easy task. In *Let Your Life Speak: Listening for the Voice of Vocation*, Parker J. Palmer elegantly expresses this difficulty: "Our strongest gifts are usually those we are barely aware of possessing. They are part of our God-given nature, with us from the moment we drew first breath, and we are no more conscious of having them than we are of breathing."

I was in my forties before I realised that one of my strengths is the capacity to quickly churn through masses of research and synthesise and articulate the core ideas. I was always aware that I read faster than most people, but it wasn't until I experienced a period where a few people commented on my research capacity, that I began to realise I possessed a strength that not everyone else had. Armed with this knowledge, I was then able to leverage that strength by intentionally developing and utilising it. This is how we excel.

In their book, *How to Be Exceptional,* Zenger, Folman, Sherwin, and Steel offer the following questions to help leaders uncover their own strengths as well those of their team members. I have added a few extra:

- Where am I most competent?
- What do I do that energises me?
- Do I have strengths in the embryo stage?
- What do I most frequently receive positive feedback about?
- What did I enjoy doing as a child?
- Where do I experience a sense of "flow"—where I am so involved in and enjoying a task that I become unaware of anything else?

What can you do?

In studying leaders in organisations, Rath and Conchie author of "Finding Your Leadership Strengths; Why Effective Leaders Must Possess a High Level of Self-Awareness," found that what made them exceptional as leaders was their individual strengths. In other words, they stood out, because their leadership style was consistent with their natural talents. It all starts with you, so here are some steps you can take:

- Get clarity about your greatest strengths.
- Set aside some time to reflect on the questions above.

- Email five people you trust, and ask them to tell you what they think your top strengths are. Remember, you are not always going to be the best judge of your own strengths, so stay open. If one person tells you you're a horse, then they are crazy, but if five people tell you you're a horse, it's time to buy a saddle!

- Set aside time with each team member to discuss the above questions. Strategise together about how they can best play to their strengths in your context.

- Encourage team members to give each other feedback when they notice strengths surfacing.

Link individual, team, and organisational goals

It's a lack of clarity that creates chaos and frustration. Those emotions are poison to any living goal.

–DR. STEVE MARABOLI, AUTHOR AND SPEAKER

The Corporate Executive Board recently completed a global study of the engagement level of 50,000 employees around the world, and number one of the top twenty-five drivers of engagement is having a clear connection between a team member's role and the overall organisational strategy. In others words, if a team member has a clear line of sight between what they do and the team and organisational goals, then they are most likely to be highly engaged. There are a couple of reasons why you as leaders need to create this connection.

Firstly, as a leader, you have a much better handle on the overall context and big picture strategy of your organisation than your team. It is easy to forget that they haven't been privy to the meetings and conversations that you have. You are the one who can connect what they do on a daily basis with higher-level goals.

Secondly, meaningful goals create hope, focus, and build confidence once those goals are attained or progress has been made. It is interesting that researchers seeking to identify strategies for creating hope in the workplace have centred on building goal-setting skills. Researchers Lock and Latham, authors of "New Directions for Goal-Setting," have found a clear connection between effective goal-setting and performance, adding that "appropriate goal-setting does not only influence one's level of motivation, choices made, effort extended, and persistence, but also the willingness and ability to design creative ways by which to achieve one's goals." By encouraging each team member to set individual goals that are linked directly to team and organisational goals, you help provide meaning and focus for your team while also allowing members to tap into their own creativity.

What can you do?

The best way to create and maintain the connections is through ongoing conversations.

Set aside time with each team member to discuss how he or she sees their individual work goals feeding into team and organisational goals. Instead of "telling" your team member how their role connects, open up a two-way conversation by asking the following kinds of questions:

- What do you see as your top 3-5 work goals?

- How do you see these goals contributing to the success of the team?

- How do you see these goals contributing to the success of the organisation?

- What specifically do you think you need to do to achieve your goals?

- What do you think it looks like when you are doing a good job?

- Are there any barriers you see to reaching your goals?

- What support or resources can I provide to help you be more successful?

Allocate time at team meetings to regularly review team goals and connect them with organisational goals. Have each team member share how their current tasks are contributing.

Regular two-way feedback

Feedback is the breakfast of champions.

–KENNETH H. BLANCHARD, AUTHOR OF *THE ONE MINUTE MANAGER*

One of Jack Canfield's Success Principles is "use feedback to your advantage," and this is certainly true in the context of a team. As Canfield notes, when you start seeking feedback, "you'll get data, advice, help, suggestions, direction, and even criticism that will help you constantly adjust and move forward while continually enhancing your knowledge, abilities, attitudes, and relationships."

Research validates the critical role feedback plays in improving performance and engagement. The Corporate Executive Board found that "of all the interactions managers can have with their employees, informal feedback has the greatest impact on enterprise contribution." Luthans and colleagues note the effectiveness of building self-confidence in the workplace through providing positive feedback. They found that "over two decades of empirical research strongly support the impact that contingently applied positive feedback and social recognition has on enhancing employees' performance, sometimes even beyond monetary rewards and other motivational techniques."

Feedback boosts engagement in two ways:

- Firstly, positive feedback has a powerful effect on self-esteem and self-confidence which increases team members' belief in their capacity to succeed, making them much more likely to do so. Frequent, informal positive feedback helps people know they are on track and acknowledges their contribution.

- Secondly, negative feedback, delivered in positive and respectful ways, helps people by providing specific information about how they can improve their performance. The problem is, while everyone loves to receive positive feedback, not everyone is so willing to hear negative feedback. Using it to build engagement often requires a shift in mindset for the leader and team members. Most people view negative or corrective feedback as "bad." It can trigger feelings of failure, rejection, not being good enough, not being liked, or having let the team down. Many of us have painful experiences of times when negative feedback was delivered in unhelpful or even harmful ways.

I remember the first piece of negative feedback I ever received at work. One day, I approached my supervisor to ask him a question. His response was to jump up from his desk and roar, "Don't (expletive, expletive) interrupt me when I am concentrating ever again!" Well, that was certainly feedback, for the whole first floor and me! I was mortified, and it left a lasting impression, but not about how I could improve my performance, and it certainly didn't increase my level of engagement.

Sadly, this event could have provided a rich source of information for me, if the feedback had been delivered differently. Imagine if his response to me had been, "I can see you are stuck, and I am in the middle of working on something critical right now, so let's catch up in an hour or so." My self-esteem would have remained intact, and I would have learned that I couldn't assume others are always available to help when it suits me. He would have experienced a much better outcome as well, as he could have calmly continued with his work. As it was, his meltdown so overwhelmed him that he stormed out, taking the rest of the day off to recover from his embarrassment.

In a team context, effective use of feedback requires a prerequisite of trust and a willingness to have real conversations, even if that means raising opposing views or uncomfortable issues. Patrick Lencioni, author of *The Five Dysfunctions of a Team*, paints a picture of what teams that trust look like, stating that they "do not hold back with one another. They are unafraid to air their dirty laundry. They admit their mistakes, their weaknesses, and their concerns without fear of reprisal." In other words, they are willing to give each other feedback, whether it is positive or negative, as they understand that it is vital information necessary to create an environment where the team feels psychologically safe and can thrive.

What can you do?

As the leader, you set the stage for how feedback is viewed in your team. Take time to prepare your feedback before you give it and consider these suggestions:

- **Demonstrate your commitment to both positive and negative feedback by giving it regularly and informally.** Communicate that you view negative feedback as information and, as Jack Canfield suggests, "improvement opportunities," rather than as something punitive or a personal attack.

- **Ask for feedback from your team members.** This powerfully models that you value feedback. Asking questions like, "What worked well in that meeting I just led?" or "What could have worked better for you?" are non-threatening invitations for your team to tell you what they think. Make sure you don't react defensively or blame others if you hear something you don't like, as that will guarantee they will never express their negative views again.

- **Ensure feedback is timely.** Unlike revenge, feedback is a dish best served warm, that is, as soon as practical after the event. However, if you are emotionally engaged, it is better to let it cool and process those emotions first. Also, if there is even a hint of negativity about it, give the feedback privately.

- **Make feedback specific.** Whether it's positive or negative, make it detailed enough for the team member to know what they did right or wrong. Just saying, "Great job!" may make someone feel good for a minute, but it is nowhere near as powerful as saying, "I really loved the way your paper addressed all the key issues," as this tells them specifically what to do more of. Similarly, if it is negative feedback, provide it with a developmental focus by stating specifically what you would like them to do next time.

- **Focus on behaviour, not personality.** Giving negative feedback is not an opportunity to engage in character assassination. Make sure you can identify behaviourally what needs to change, and communicate clearly the behaviours you expect. Adopt a coaching approach by noticing behaviours and asking questions. So, instead of making comments like, "You are so negative lately," try, "I noticed in our meeting yesterday, that most of your comments were critical. Are you okay with where we are heading?" This opens up a conversation that is more likely to provide real information you can both work with.

- **Make feedback a team event.** Try this activity that I often run with teams, adapted from a family tradition I instituted when my four sons were young. We called it, "One thing I like..." and occasionally, after dinner, we would go around the table, taking turns to say one thing we liked about each person. In a team setting, each person identifies two things they like, and one thing that would work better, about each person. Allow people a few minutes to prepare individually and remind them to focus on behaviours when it comes to what could work better. Allow adequate time and enjoy the powerful moments you will experience as a team.

Where to from here?

How could you have a soccer team if all were goalkeepers?
How would it be an orchestra if all were French horns?

—BISHOP DESMOND TUTU, SOCIAL RIGHTS ACTIVIST

Your team is a set of unique individuals, with differing strengths, goals, hopes, and passions who most likely want to be happy and excel at their work. Yet, the research makes it clear that very few people are performing anywhere near their potential. As a leader, you have the opportunity to make a difference by focusing on what we know are the key drivers for engagement, and thereby creating a team that people want to be a part of.

Depending on the state of your team, you might just need a little tweaking, or perhaps you need a major overhaul. It doesn't matter where you are; the critical thing is that you start. Take an honest look at how engaged your team members are. Have conversations with them. Use the suggestions in this chapter, make a plan, and take action. Your team will thank you, and so will your leaders, as your team begins to shine.

Bibliography

Buckingham & Coffman, *First Break all the Rules: What the World's Greatest Managers Do Differently*, Simon & Schuster, UK, 2005.

Canfield, Jack. *The Success Principles: How to Get from Where You are to Where You Want to Be*, HarperCollins, NY, 2005.

Corporate Executive Board, *Managing for Enterprise Contribution: Ten Imperatives for Managing in the New Work Environment*, 2012.

Edmonson, Amy. *The Fearless Organization: Creating Psychological Safety in the Workplace for Learning, Innovation and Growth*, Wiley, New Jersey, 2019

Gallup, *State of the Global Workforce*, 2013.

Lencioni, P., *The Five Dysfunctions of a Team: A Leadership Fable*, Jossey-Bass, San Francisco, 2002.

Locke, Edwin A.; Latham, Gary P. "New Directions for Goal-Setting," *Current Directions in Psychological Science* (Wiley-Blackwell). Vol. 15 Issue 5, (2006). 265–268.

Luthans, F., Youseff, C. M. & Avolio, B. J., *Psychological Capital: Developing the Human Competitive Edge*, Oxford University Press, Oxford, 2007.

Pryce-Jones, J., *Happiness at Work: Maximizing Your Psychological Capital for Success*, Wiley-Blackwell, UK, 2010.

Parker J. Palmer, *Let Your Life Speak: Listening for the Voice of Vocation,* Jossey- Bass, San Francisco, 2000.

Rath, T; Conchie, B. "Finding Your Leadership Strengths; Why Effective Leaders Must Possess a High Level of Self-Awareness." *Gallup Management Journal.* Gallup Organization, 2008.

Scott, Susan *Fierce Leadership: A Bold Alternative to the Worst 'Best Practices' of Business Today.* Little, Brown Book Group, New York. Kindle Edition. 2010.

Stajkovic, A. D., & Luthans, F. "A Meta-Analysis of the Effects of Organizational Behavior Modification on Task Performance." *Academy of Management Journal,* (1997), 40, 1122–1149.

Walumbwa, F. O., Luthans, F., Avey, J. B. and Oke, A., "Authentically Leading Groups: The Mediating Role of Collective Psychological Capital and Trust." *Journal of Organizational Behavior,* (2011),32: 4–24. doi: 10.1002/job.653

Zenger, J. H., Folkman, J. R., Sherwin, R. H., Steel, B. A., *How to Be Exceptional,* McGraw Hill, New York, 2012.

Sally Dooley is a highly engaging and experienced facilitator, speaker, and executive coach. During her twenty-year career, Sally has worked with thousands of leaders in government, private, and community sectors, specializing in a wide range of leadership and people development areas. Her own experience in leading teams has given her an in-depth understanding of the current issues and challenges facing leaders, as well as the capacity to empower leaders to identify strategies that work in their own contexts so they can create teams that shine.

Sally draws on techniques from design thinking and improvisation to create learning environments where people are supported to think creatively and show up as their best selves. She is also a highly sought-after speaker and is known for her capacity to build powerful rapport with her audiences, and balance inspiration with practical take-aways.

In addition, Sally is especially passionate about helping women leaders identify and break through their individual barriers so they can lead with excellence and reach their highest potential. Her *Lead Well Aim High* program has helped many women leaders take positive steps toward achieving their leadership goals.

Sally has a master's in Training and Development, and a strong commitment to professional excellence, which includes a twelve-month Train the Trainer program with Jack Canfield. She is a TEDx speaker and speaker coach.

Her website is www.sallydooley.com

CHAPTER 7

Leadership at the Heart Level
Embracing and Implementing Change to Bring Meaningful Visions to Life

by Jaroslav Průša

Leadership is a magnificent adventure that brings about feelings of success and deep fulfillment but also moments of frustration, uncertainty, and fear. Strong emotions and empowering mindsets are the keys to people's behavior and performance. Effective leaders know how to leverage these qualities in themselves and in other people to bring their visions and strategies to life. By choosing the right approach, they harness natural energy and the potential of everyday situations and facilitate desired changes in people's attitudes and behavior in real time.

They connect at the heart level—from the heart of a leader to the hearts of the people they lead—and by no means is this an easy task.

Where I Began

My personal discovery of this heart-level approach to leadership started in the mid-nineties, when I worked with a global leader in healthcare as a regional product manager and later as a marketing director for Central and Eastern Europe for one of its product divisions. Our challenge was to move from insignificant market share to a clear leadership position in key markets of the region that spread from the Czech Republic in the West to Russia in the East, and from Poland in the North to Croatia in the South.

In order to guarantee long-term profitable growth across the range of diverse countries, we needed a regional strategy and a group of local divisional managers who would implement this approach in their respective markets. My personal challenge was to unite these managers into a productive team and lead the transition. I had to learn to lead changes through relationships built on mutual trust, respect, and responsibility.

However, we had a rather bumpy start. When all managers from the region met and agreed to work together, I believed that we were ready to go. What a naïve thought! My leadership journey had barely started. Our first step was to develop a simple reporting process. The managers agreed to provide me with their country sales information. I designed a simple form and sent it to them with a deadline. That's when I hit the wall. There were no objections or questions to my request, so I was pleased at how smoothly everything was going—except that there was no response before the deadline either. A sense of uncertainty began to creep in. What would happen if I were late with putting together the regional report? How would I look? Are they testing me? My mind generated a number of interpretations and catastrophic scenarios.

As I became aware of what was happening, I stopped, relaxed, and turned inside. A pivotal idea that it was me who was responsible slipped into my consciousness. It was in my hands whether or not our regional vision would come to life. So, I put on my selling hat and began to see the managers as my clients. I became interested in them as individuals, and I asked myself: What kind of situation are they in? How do they see this request and the ultimate change in business practices from their perspective? What are their needs and desires?

Once I put myself in their shoes, the picture changed dramatically. The clarity I gained was striking. I decided to meet each of them where they were at that moment and use this emotionally triggered situation as a natural doorway to building mutually cooperative relationships. This single change in perspective became the main turning point. The moment I changed my own mindset, the right solution became apparent. As I became aware of and understood their needs and desires, the managers relaxed their defenses and joined me.

From that point on, we still had to resolve many issues, alter our ways of thinking, and develop new skills. But it was worth the effort. Over six years, our regional strategy was successfully implemented, and our market share in core markets moved from less than 5% up to over 50%. Our sales force became the new industry standard in terms of confidence, customer relationships, and sales performance. We even designed a new concept of advanced sales training that was adopted by other European countries.

During this process, I learned the following lessons:

- It all starts with stepping into personal power to meet the challenge.

- Having an appealing vision and a simple strategy to bring it to life is vital.

- Changes must occur in people's minds, hearts, and actions; the essence of leadership is to gain people's trust and cooperation, and provide them with guidance, encouragement, and support they need to succeed.

- Getting things done requires effective infrastructures and consistency in following through.

- When leading people into the unknown, we set clear intentions, get moving, see what happens, get feedback, and learn quickly from our experience, then adjust our approach and continue until we succeed.

The Need for a Paradigm Change

Since 2008, the situations in many organizations have fundamentally changed. Despite all their efforts, it has been increasingly difficult for many managers to effectively deal with the challenges they face. Experience shows that in order to cope with the growing demands, many of them use too much force or, conversely, are not attentive and consistent enough in leading people.

> *By choosing the right approach, they [leaders] harness natural energy and the potential of everyday situations and facilitate desired changes in people's attitudes and behavior in real time.*

However, nothing is more counterproductive than unnecessary top-down pressure that produces uncertainty, anxiety, and fear, and results in long-term stress, bottom-up obedience (or resistance), and mediocre results. On the other hand, managers' insufficient attention and consistency leave room for dilution of responsibility and morale, slow implementation of important projects, and again only average results.

So, how can we lead people to assume responsibility, become pro-active, self-reliant, and motivated, keep learning, acquire new skills, and bring their work to higher levels? Actually, it may be simpler than we think, but it requires more than we usually do.

Creating Space for People to Succeed and Grow

The road to success and better results requires a change in our attitude to leadership and implementing change in organizations. As leaders we need to move away from excessive pressure, toxic stress, and fear, or insufficient attention and consistency, toward greater mutual trust, respect, and understanding. Active engagement of each individual and responsibility for the overall outcome is vital. This will give us the leverage we need to enlist the minds and hearts of people and fully utilise their natural talents and creative potential.

Instead of trying to control everything:

- Let's bring change to the front line where it naturally belongs. Let's create a safe, inspiring, and empowering environment where people can enter without fear, and actively engage in the realization of a common vision while using their natural talents, enjoying success and continuing their professional and personal growth.

- Let's learn to pay attention to what is happening within and around us and use both everyday situations and the life-changing events to guide people's attitudes and actions. Let's choose the right leadership style that will enable us to take advantage of the natural energy and potential of the situation and keep moving in the desired direction.

- And last, but not least, let's also become comfortable in leading a constant stream of mutually interacting changes. Being in it together with people we aspire to lead, but letting them create, make their own decisions, and learn from their mistakes and successes—that is the way to develop upcoming leaders who are needed at all levels of business and other organizations.

As a result, we will be able to bring our visions to life more easily and with much better outcomes.

Leadership at the Heart Level: Five Core Elements

In order to bring a meaningful vision to life, leadership becomes hands-on, day-to-day, shoulder-to-shoulder work with—and for—the people that a leader aspires to lead. It is daily attention to initiating, facilitating, and anchoring changes in attitudes and behavior. It is about helping others overcome roadblocks they face, moving through the change process effectively, enjoying the victory, and learning from personal experience.

During the past few decades, I have come to realize that truly effective leaders master the following five core elements of leadership:

1. Courage to Act in Face of Ambiguity, Uncertainty, and Risk

Leaders face major challenges, be it disappointing performance in a slow economy, radical changes in customer demands or purchasing behavior, or new change initiatives from headquarters. They need to have the courage to act and find solutions in face of ambiguity, uncertainty, and risk.

The key purpose of the first element is to get moving and find answers to the central question: "What can we do about the situation?" Therefore, courageous leaders:

- See challenging situations as opportunities for major improvement.
- Trust their abilities, speak up, and fight for their ideas.
- Have the courage to go beyond established practices and try new approaches.
- Come up with creative ideas and identify a number of alternative solutions.
- Act decisively, evoking a sense of urgency.

Leadership Experience 1: A core part of our regional strategy was using one specific business segment as a pilot project that would serve as a platform for developing processes and skills for long-term profitable growth and building a strong leadership team along the way. In order to draft an appealing vision and effective strategy for attaining it, we needed to understand the market situation and customers' needs first. So, I initiated a quick market research. Being concerned about additional workload, the local managers were not too excited about the idea.

However, after I spoke with each of them one-on-one, addressing their concerns, using their ideas, and showing easy ways of approaching the task, their initial resistance quickly turned into willing cooperation. In just four weeks, we had compiled data from ten key accounts in each sales territory in the region. Wow! The results demonstrated that joint regional projects could be implemented quickly and efficiently. It built confidence and trust. This direct experience triggered a significant change in attitudes and behavior, and it prepped the leadership team for the launch of a regional strategy that happened two months later.

2. Setting Direction Through Vision and Strategy

The key purpose of the second element is to determine where we want to go and how we get there—the vision of a desired future and the strategy for achieving it. Decisive leaders:

- Stay focused on their purpose while maintaining a helicopter point-of-view.

- Formulate a meaningful vision that unites and mobilizes people to determined action.

- Think in alternatives and consult feasibility of alternative approaches with key stakeholders.

- Make responsible decisions in the highest long-term interest of all involved.

- Have the heart to lead the way and fight for what is right.

Leadership Experience 2: Once we had obtained essential data through our market research, we streamlined our product portfolio with a clear upgrading structure for long-term profitable growth, agreed upon marketing support tools, introduced a new concept of customer education, drafted an outline for a regional training summit, put together bonus schemes, and agreed upon regular progress reviews. While drafting all the key parts of the strategy, I kept consulting with each manager one-on-one. Then, we met as a team and agreed upon the whole package. Three things were instrumental to our success:

- We had to stay focused on our prime goal and reinforcing the focus during all our communication.

- A meaningful vision with a clear-cut pragmatic strategy must be held by all.

- Involving all managers in decision-making allowed each manager to be a part of the game, fully understand the plan and their role, and assume their responsibility for the team results.

By using the energy generated during the market research and leading the process with a clear goal in mind, everything fell into place very naturally. In less than a month, the vision and strategy were set. We then faced the challenge of enlisting support and cooperation from the whole sales force. We were about to have a lot of fun!

3. Enlisting Support and Willing Cooperation

Leaders enlist the support and willing cooperation of those who will participate in the implementation of set visions and strategies.

Our vision needs to become a shared vision that people believe in, identify with, and are willing to fight for. That is the essence of the third element.

In selling their message inside and outside their organizations, leaders build relationships, inspire trust, confidence, and commitment, and create empowering environments for people to step in with power, succeed, and grow. Therefore, responsible leaders:

- Explain the vision, its meaning and benefits, and the role people will play in its implementation, repeatedly.
- Ask people for their opinion, answer questions, and involve them in planning.
- Build on common interests, addressing legitimate needs and desires of major interest groups.
- Are sincerely interested in people as individuals, their views, ideas, and performance.
- Teach people to score goals by providing training, encouragement, and support.

Leadership Experience 3: When enlisting support for our regional strategy, holding a regional training summit was another crucial step in working together, this time with—and in front of—the entire sales force from the region. There was a lot at stake! All of the managers were involved in the program preparation and played active roles during its execution. They led some of the presentations and play activities, participated in role-playings, and ran satellite meetings with their teams speaking their local languages, discussing implementation of regional strategy in their local environment, asking questions, and bringing key issues back to be answered for the whole group. They became the champions for change. Three months after we began working together, we succeeded in setting direction for the region, aligning the leadership team behind a shared vision, and the entire sales force was trained, confident, inspired, and ready to go. We were about to face the moment of truth.

4. Following Through to Get Results

As we enlist the minds and hearts of people, we need to shift attention and energy into ensuring that what needs to be done gets done. The essence of the fourth element is keeping the vision at the center of attention, observing and reinforcing compliance with set directions, guidelines, and procedures, and following through to successful completion. Consistent leaders:

- Design effective systems and processes while keeping things simple.
- Observe and reinforce compliance with set directions, guidelines, and procedures.
- Monitor progress against plans and provide timely feedback.
- Promote respect and responsibility for team results and provide sincere recognition and rewards for a job well done.
- Openly share their experience and best practices.

Leadership Experience 4: When bringing the highest quality products into the region, it was important for our customers to understand and appreciate the differences in quality. Introducing the new concept of customer education was instrumental to our success. We introduced the idea to my home market first, and after several runs, we refined the concept. We rolled it out during the regional training summit so that all managers and sales representatives had direct hands-on experience. Then it was time to launch the concept in other countries, and a launch timeline was agreed upon. However, the manager who was to be the first to implement it showed a tendency to postpone the dates. It was clear that the first implementation of the program outside my home market (or the lack of it) would send an important message to the other countries. I had to face the challenge head-on. During our conversation, I noticed that the manager's confidence and motivation were running low. I had to remain friendly, yet firm. I decided to involve the country manager and assert the idea through formal authority.

At the same time, I made myself available to assist the local team in the workshop preparation and joined them during the first run in order to provide guidance, support, and feedback. The workshop became a major success; customers were enthusiastic and the local team grew confident and motivated. What a relief! I shared the success story with all of the other managers and publicly praised the local team for their work and job well done. Sales skyrocketed. Other countries joined in and asked for support. For several months, I travelled across the region to share best practices and support local teams during their launches. Regular progress reviews enabled managers to benchmark their performance against other countries, and the sales soared.

5. Learning from Experience

Leaders know the importance of pausing and reflecting upon their experience to develop deeper understanding of how successful they have really been. The essence of this fifth element is raising our awareness of reality and learning from experience. Humble leaders:

- Take time to evaluate the situation in a wider context of the overall intention.
- Have the courage to face reality.
- Appraise performance of teams and individuals and identify priorities for improvement.
- Get feedback on their own effectiveness as leaders.
- Formulate specific lessons learned at personal and organizational levels.

Leadership Experience 5: Quarterly progress reviews and evaluations of the strategy implementation helped us learn and make timely adjustments. Everybody was able to see that the new approach worked. This was critical as we were entering a new business planning cycle where were we able to demonstrate tangible results and steep sales growth in the pilot segment in comparison to other segments. Our approach became a template for other segments. However, the all-important achievement was that, in less than a year, we had laid a solid foundation for fast growing long-term profitable business and built a leadership team that would drive it.

Making It Work

These five elements may seem simple at first, and actually, they really are. The challenge is how we employ them in specific situations and from which mindset we operate. The following seven core principles of Leadership at the Heart Level helped us harness the natural energy of each challenging situation and bring our vision to life.

Principle 1: Raising the Level of Awareness

Change happens in the present moment by staying fully present and paying attention to what is happening within and around us. Becoming truly aware of self, others, and the situation allows us to make conscious choices and navigate each situation to its desired outcome. By taking time after the situation to pause and reflect, we can learn from personal experience and intentionally adjust our approach.

Principle 2: Respecting the Natural Flow of Energy

When sailing, we cannot change the wind, but we can adjust the sails. Similarly, as leaders we can only work with the situations at hand, welcoming whatever comes, dealing with it as best as we can, and learning from our experience. Leaders trust that the situation is just perfect as it is and that they have all they need to deal with it successfully. They see opportunities and harness their inherent energy and potential.

Principle 3: Meeting People Where They Are

In order for their people to succeed, effective leaders provide them with what they need to be better prepared for the job at hand. By being aware of the actual state of mind, feelings, and emotions of their team members, leaders can facilitate necessary changes in people's attitudes and behavior in real time. By meeting people where they are at the moment, leaders are able to help them move to the next level of performance.

Principle 4: Implementing Sustainable Solutions

In today's turbulent business environment, corporations need to move to greater stability and sustainability. However, when facing major challenges, far too many managers have a pain-avoiding tendency for quick-fix solutions. Speed, and the need to demonstrate their strength, has become the name of the game. No matter how quickly the managers act and how strong they may appear, they simply miss the mark. Quick-fix solutions usually address only the symptoms of a problem, not its root causes. The problems keep reappearing and produce additional challenges. Effective leaders understand broader context, focus on addressing the root causes of an issue, and implement solutions that are sustainable in the long term.

Principle 5: Making Responsible Choices in the Highest Interest of All

In order to bring our visions to life, we need to create space for others to join us. We need support and cooperation from a wide range of interest groups—our teams and colleagues, managers, people from headquarters, investors, communities, suppliers, and customers. So, we need to understand, respect, and address the legitimate needs and interests of all these groups. Is it simple? No! Is it important? Yes! Effective leaders build on common interests and often fight for greater causes that go beyond mere personal interests and their comfort zone.

Principle 6: Building Relationships on Mutual Trust, Respect, and Responsibility

In order to succeed in an increasingly complex and dynamic business environment, we need to take advantage of the expertise, talents, and energy of each individual by bringing people together and allowing the synergy of teamwork to happen. We bring out the best in people when we build relationships on mutual trust, respect, and responsibility. When we create safe, inspirational, and empowering work environments in which people can use their unique talents and passions, we repeatedly succeed and grow while bringing meaningful visions to life. Leaders treat themselves and others with respect, dignity, and love, knowing that being human is more important than any business goal or result.

Principle 7: Walking Tall

Leadership is more about who you are than what your position is. It is you that people follow, not your role or title. Be grounded in who you really are: authentic and consistent in your words and actions. A leader's credibility is rooted in the set of ethical values he or she believes in, and in his or her personal integrity in living them every day. Responsibility, desire to serve, continuous learning and improvement, humanity, and compassion are values most critical to a leader's success. By being clear about personal values and living them, leaders not only develop greater trust and rapport with others, but they also model the way people follow.

When we embrace these principles, moving beyond mere intellectual understanding to receiving them on an emotional and spiritual level, they become an integral part of our being and form a rock-solid foundation for our leadership. We are then ready to successfully navigate our organization through challenging times.

> *When we create safe, inspirational, and empowering work environments in which people can use their unique talents and passions, we repeatedly succeed and grow while bringing meaningful visions to life..*

A Call to Action

The magic of Leadership at the Heart Level is that it actually works! Shortly after implementing our regional strategy, I used the same approach to turn around a declining business division from -17% to +24% growth in just twelve months. When teaching the concept, one of my first clients increased their quarterly sales by 86% year-on-year and another gained five percentage points in a mature market! Others reported new business opportunities, reduced costs, improved service levels, and major increases in confidence, credibility, contentment, and inner calm.

How can *you* benefit? You can start by looking at opportunities for improvement in three simple steps:

Step 1: On a scale of 1-10 (10 being "Completely Satisfied"), how would you rate your level of satisfaction with the current situation in the organization you lead in the following areas:

1. Business results
2. Courage to act and find solutions in face of ambiguity, uncertainty, and risk
3. Setting direction through vision and strategy

4. Enlisting support and willing cooperation

5. Following through to get results

6. Learning from experience

Step 2: In areas where your assessment was less than 10, ask yourself "What would it take to make it a 10?" The answers are your key opportunities for development.

Step 3: After reviewing all six areas, how do you plan to improve the situation? List three to five main action steps:

_____

_____

_____

_____

_____

Congratulations! You have just taken the first step toward getting better results and enjoying higher levels of satisfaction in what you do.

Jaroslav Průša is an experienced leadership and executive coach with over thirty years of business, managerial, and coaching experience in the environment of global corporations.

He inspires and supports managers in *dealing with challenging situations* and *embracing change*, accelerating their *personal and professional growth*, and *developing the next generation of business leaders.*

With a postgraduate degree in management from Technology University of Prague, Czech Republic, and an MBA from University of Northumbria at Newcastle, UK, he completed a year-long Train the Trainer program with Jack Canfield and also became a Master RIM° Facilitator and a RIM° Trainer.

He designed and led programs for organizations, like ABB, AstraZeneca, Biogen, Citibank, Toyota, and The Office of the

Czech Republic Government. He has also taught leadership and change in an MBA in Healthcare program for eleven years.

Jaroslav's fundamentally new approach to leadership and leadership development has become a foundation for several original transformational programs. For more information please visit www.jaroslavprusa.cz

CHAPTER 8

How to Outfox the Three Subconscious Saboteurs Lurking in Your Workplace

by Jane Ransom

When business owners learn I'm a brain-trainer and a master hypnotist, they ask one of two things. The wording varies, but it's basically either 1) Can I turn them into a chicken? or 2) Can I help get them or their people to perform better (because right now they're paralyzed by inner gridlock, or de-energized by apathy, or willpower-less, or couldn't come up with a creative idea if the survival of all humankind depended on it—which by the way it kinda does)?

Either way, the answer is "Yes."

That's because, besides being a hypnotist, I'm also a science nerd with a powerful set of Self-Intelligence®, mix-n-match, brain-training tools to pry people out of their ruts.

Most of those ruts are forms of subconscious self-sabotage. Typically, people know they're stuck, but they don't know why (since by definition the subconscious remains hidden from conscious awareness), and that not-knowing can make folks feel foolish, confused, frustrated, and all the more stuck. This is about as fun as finding yourself in a six-lane traffic jam when you meant to be taking a shortcut because you were already running late. I help lift people out of their gridlock, so they can reach their goals faster.

Fortunately, science today provides many strategies to combat subconscious sabotage. This is big news. When I was growing up, the term "subconscious" got about as much respect as ghost sightings, paranormal spoon-bending, or pulling rabbits out of hats. Fascinating stuff for fifth-graders, but not really suited for corporate meetings.

However, scientists worldwide are now studying the subconscious, and business leaders are taking note. Just the other day, an MBA-program professor asked me to serve on a panel of experts exploring how to program the subconscious brain for success. The reason for this new focus is that computer-driven neuro-imaging technology has wrought a revolution in neuroscience. One key finding is that it's our subconscious brain that generally runs the show. Some people find this painful to accept, as it's a bit like being told that it's your invisible friend, and not you, who makes the big decisions around here. Fortunately, another key finding is that we can strategically redirect the subconscious to get what we consciously want. All of this has to do with the discovery of neuroplasticity, also called brain plasticity. What scientists discovered is that your brain is a shape-shifter.

Back in the pre-plasticity stone age, scientists still believed that the adult brain was unchangeable, as if by age twenty-five, every brain-thing about you—from your personality to your IQ, to whether or not you were talented at golf or guitar or pulling rabbits from hats—was virtually set in stone. Now we know the opposite is true. Now we know that throughout your life you can significantly change and improve your brain. However, that won't happen on its own any more than your dog is going to start organizing your sock drawer. To reform your brain, or the brains of people who work for you, you have to know how to train the subconscious. That's where I can help you (not so much with your dog).

To vanquish our foes, we must first identify them, which can be tricky with subconscious phenomena. Not only is your subconscious brain activity hidden from your conscious mind, but most of it is friendly, not enemy-ish at all. Your subconscious keeps you alive and functional. Here's one small example: All day long, whether you're leading a meeting, riding in an airplane, or having a bowl of soup, you go around with your head held up, without even thinking about it. Yet, if all forms of consciousness suddenly were knocked out of you, your head would fall sideways, onto the shoulder of the passenger beside you, or down into your soup bowl. Your subconscious holds your head up for you. So, usually the correct attitude is: Thank you, subconscious!

Usually, but not always. Sometimes destructive tendencies can sneak into our brains, and we only know they're there from the damage they do. At the office, this can show up as disengagement, lack of willpower, low energy, creative blocks, or other forms of loserness. It won't help to attack these outward effects. In each case, we must conquer the culprit cause.

So, here are three of the most common and costly subconscious saboteurs lurking in today's workforce (all of which will be easily defeatable once you have the brain-training tactics I'm about to give you):

1. Willpower-crushing shame.
2. A paralyzing belief left over from the pre-twenty-first century stone age that talent and IQ are fixed, as in unchangeable.
3. Dementor-type negativity threatening to drain the life-force from you.

Oh, and by the way, remember that I can turn people in chickens? You're going to learn how to do that too. So, keep reading.

1. The First Saboteur: Sneaky Shame—What the Hell?!

Have you noticed how popular shame is nowadays? Everywhere you turn, someone's wagging a shame finger at someone else—who then puts their own finger into the air, either to shame-wag back or signal hostility in some other way—and around and around it goes. This circular negativity machine is digging us all deeper and deeper into the pit of paralyzing shame.

Shaming would work if the subconscious were like your pet dog, learning from such punishment to stop eating your socks (and color-sort them already!), yet continuing to wriggle all over with joy at the very sight of you. Sadly, however, the subconscious is often more like a dimwitted, over-sensitive giant, who can't help but overpower our little conscious selves, and who, alas, is not particularly far-sighted in its thinking.

How does this big ol' giant respond to shame? Pretty much by sobbing into its giant handkerchief that all is lost, that there's no more hope of anything getting any better ever again, and therefore, instead of changing your behavior (whether that was missing deadlines, swigging too much rum, or being about as productive as a broken pencil stub), it feels compelled to carry on exactly as before, or worse.

Scientists call this the *what-the-hell effect*. It has been tested and retested, validated and verified. It's real. Stanford psychologist Kelly McGonigal calls it "one of the biggest threats to willpower worldwide"—yep, that big.

It was given its name by weight-loss researchers who were surprised to find that the more ashamed someone felt about overeating once, the more likely they were to do it again (and again and again). Further studies showed the same to be true for overdrinking, procrastinating, and pretty much any mistake involving a lapse in self-discipline. You see, making a mistake feels bad enough, but then if we pile shame on top, the subconscious goes, "Oh, now I can't bear it. I feel so terrible. There's no hope; all is lost. Oh well, since all is lost anyway, I might as well just go on repeating that awful mistake, because—" and here it shrugs its enormous shoulders while blinking its tear-filled eyes— "What the hell?"

At least that's what scientists hypothesize it thinks. In any case, the effect is well proven. The results are measurable, but the self-sabotage occurs at a subconscious level, meaning we're all vulnerable. Business leaders need to know about this. First, because many leaders are hard on themselves, piling on self-criticism without realizing the harm it does—i.e. the reason they're limping is because they keep shooting themselves in the proverbial foot. Second, research shows that workers are super-sensitive to feedback from higher-ups. So, what may seem to you like helpful correction when you deliver it, may feel to your employee's subconscious as though you've sucker-punched them in the gut.

At that point (and again, subconsciously), the what-the-hell effect will take over, making it even harder for them to do better next time, leading to more anxiety, more mistakes, more criticism, and more loss of morale (both theirs and presumably yours).

All is lost! Or it would be, if we didn't have a way to crush this enemy. Scientists have found one, but it's so simple that you might not believe me, so let me first share a story.

When Ben arrived at my office, he called himself a "fat, lazy slob" and "pathetic bum." He said: "I bought a gym membership four months ago, and haven't gone once." His beer belly was pushing so urgently against his shirt that it looked as though at any moment a button or two might take flight. Ben wanted me to help him lose weight, but he also was having other problems, including with his company, a biz-to-biz delivery service. He crew was slacking off—showing up late, losing packages, offending customers, and generally making clear they didn't give a hoot.

Maybe you noticed the way Ben spoke about himself wasn't all that nice. He didn't know it, but he had been, for quite some time, inducing the what-the-hell effect in his own subconscious by shaming himself. This had nothing to do with being wimpy. Ben was tough. He'd fought in Vietnam. After the war, he'd built his business from scratch. Most of his employees were veterans as well.

They were tough, too. For many years, his crew and he had enjoyed a profitable relationship of mutual respect.

But when, in middle age, his waistline began to widen, here's what Ben did, because it's natural: He started berating himself. The more self-critical he grew, the more he criticized everyone else, and the more demoralized they became. Pretty soon, he was growing big as a tank while his business was tanking. Ben needed to deactivate the what-the-hell effect.

Are you ready? Here's the science-proven solution: Self-forgiveness.

Researchers have found that even a little self-pep talk can pull a person right out of hell and back on track with their lives. This can be as simple as saying to yourself (out loud or silently), "Hey me! Everybody makes mistakes. It's okay. We're not meant to be perfect. My dear self, I forgive you."

That may sound silly, but remember: our subconscious can be a dufus. When it hears this pep talk, it reasons, "Wait a minute—I'm still loved, cherished, and respected?! I had no idea. This changes everything. I'm not forever doomed after all. There's hope, hope, hope!" *Voilà*—willpower restored, behavior improved, results measurable.

While studies show even a single dose of self-forgiveness can create immediate results, to kick the self-shaming habit requires long-term commitment. So, Ben had to practice. And while we were cleaning out the garage of his mind, we found several moldy suitcases full of old guilt from the past, so we did a full spring-clean, as it were. Ben recovered his willpower, his health, and his self-esteem. Then, he had some new forgiveness skills to help his crew shape up as well. They regained their work ethic.

Here's how you too can save yourself and your company from the what-the-hell effect:

- Let's start with you. Is there any area of your life that could use more self-discipline? If you're short on willpower, odds are you're long on shame. Either start giving yourself some serious anti-shame pep talks, or go download my free *Forgive Thyself* audio from self-intelligence.com.

- Are your employees people? Well then, they're going to make mistakes. Turn those into truly teachable moments, not just by telling them how to do things right next time, but by letting them know it's okay to be human. For extra measure, sprinkle in some praise—but beware. Certain forms of praise can be weirdly destructive, so keep reading.

2. The Fixed-Mindset Saboteur: Talent & Smarts— Kick 'Em Out!

First a quick review. We've learned how criticism (delivered by self-talk or someone else) can trigger the what-the-hell effect, wherein shame keeps on replicating like some slime-dripping tentacled sci-fi alien that also hunts down and devours self-discipline. This can happen, because our subconscious is bigger than we are, yet can be such a wuss that it throws in the towel at the slightest threat to its pride. On the other hand, because our brains are so malleable (they're so-called *plastic*, remember?), all it takes is a spoonful of self-forgiveness to get our big oaf back on track—and then a regular habit of self-forgiveness to keep us on track.

Now that we've got that sorted out, it'll be easier to wrap your head around this next strange-but-true scientific finding which by now also has been proven, re-proven, corroborated, and confirmed up the scientific wazoo, and that is: You should never praise anyone for being *smart* or *talented*.

That's right—never.

If you're ever even tempted to do so, then please picture yourself in a spooky movie where you're about to enter the basement. The basement door looks inviting, and you can't hear the audience screaming, "Nooo!" Please don't do it. Therein lurks your second deadly saboteur: the fixed mindset.

Granted, the name "fixed mindset" isn't too scary; maybe our scriptwriters can do better—or maybe they can't, because maybe they've already been turned into zombies. Creatives are the first to fall victim in this plotline. So, if the success of your organization depends on creativity (which these days whose doesn't?), listen up.

Stanford psychologist Carol Dweck was among the first to discover that praising someone as smart or talented implants a

> *You should never praise anyone for being smart or talented. When we praise someone for being smart or talented, we infect their subconscious with a fixed mindset, and despite our best intentions, this destroys their genuine confidence.*

fixed mindset. That praise activates a dormant belief, one that we humans have been harboring for, well, millennia, which is that talent and intelligence are innate, DNA-driven, inherited, permanently fixed traits. That false notion was born from the bigger false notion we've already talked about here, the old belief that our brains were virtually set in stone. (That's why I call those times the stone age, heh.) We humans have embraced this myth for so long, that it may take your subconscious a while to either acknowledge it or let go of it. To help you, here's a quick quiz. For each one of the following statements, decide whether you mostly agree or mostly disagree:

1. Your intelligence and talent are very basic things about you that you can't change much.

2. You can learn new stuff, but you can't really change how intelligent or talented you are.

3. No matter how much intelligence or talent you have, you can change them quite a bit.

4. You can always substantially change how intelligent and talented you are.

If you sided with 1 and 2, you've got a fixed mindset (which is common, given its history—but dangerous enough to call for some subconscious surgery). If instead, 3 and 4 got your vote, then you have the opposite, a growth mindset—congrats! But even then, to protect the people you lead, you must understand that praise is a double-edged sword.

When we praise someone for being smart or talented, we infect their subconscious with a fixed mindset, and despite our best intentions, this destroys their genuine confidence. Research by scientists across the globe—with students, athletes, performance artists, and businesspeople—reveals both that:

- Specifically praising intelligence or talent triggers the fixed mindset.

- Those individuals then become subconsciously terrified of doing anything that could cast doubt on their supposed superiority. Even worse, their fear is subconscious, controlling their behavior without them being consciously aware of it.

So, they resist learning new skills, because appearing even momentarily inept might suggest they're not talented or smart after all. They avoid trying too hard, because having to work at something represents to them a lack of natural ability. I've helped numerous clients conquer creative blocks, and every time what's blocking them is a fixed mindset. The paralysis they experience makes them feel like the walking dead, but being accustomed to creativity, at least they're savvy enough to know something's wrong. More often, this plague hides undiagnosed in the workplace, because its worst victims don't know they're afflicted, yet will go to extremes, even lying and cheating, to look successful, because their self-image depends on it.

Just reading the research can be frightening, but fortunately once again scientists have found a surprisingly simple antidote. In order to turn things around, not merely evicting the fixed mindset but replacing it with the opposite, a growth mindset, we must use the other side of that double-edged sword. Instead of praising people as intelligent or talented—concepts that promote an inane idea of effortless success—we praise them for effort, and we teach them about neuroplasticity.

We explain to them the facts: Now that high-tech machines allow scientists to see what's going on inside our heads, we know we can literally reform our brains. We can re-arrange the connections among our 100 billion thinking cells, called neurons. By strategically choosing better thoughts, actions and experiences, we can significantly improve our own brains.

By teaching others about plasticity, and by praising them for effort—i.e. not for who they supposedly are, but for what they actually do—we implant in them a growth mindset. This makes them proud to work hard and unafraid to take risks. It turns them into flexible learners, dedicated doers and energized creators. It's as if the subconscious goes, "What?! I can exercise my brain to grow bigger, better, stronger, and faster? So, give me a challenge already! Throw me some feedback. Show me a stretch. Let's go, let's go, let's go!" Foster a growth mindset among your people, and they will amaze you.

3. The Third Saboteur: That Killjoy You'd Like to Ignore (But Can't)

All right, but what about that one nay-saying, stick-in-the-mud, negativity-addicted blockhead who loves to bring everybody down: Have you ever had to put up with one of those? I thought so. Fear not. I'm about to share with you a secret technique from my hypnosis training.

Keep reading, because even if you consciously try to ignore that whiner who downpours on every parade and whose very presence threatens to drain the life force from you, your subconscious won't ignore them. It can't. Deep in the subconscious brain are special cells called mirror neurons that automatically "catch" other people's emotions—a handy skill, but alas, this also means that negativity is contagious. Maybe you've noticed how fast it spreads nowadays on social media. You don't want a negativity epidemic killing off your company's morale. Your people take their emotional cues from you. As a leader, you personally can't afford to catch the bleh. You must inoculate yourself against the negative knucklehead.

Of course, I'm assuming you would've fired them already if you could have. Perhaps they're a valuable asset, or your biggest customer, or maybe your boss. No problem. When people learn I'm a master hypnotist, they often ask, "Are you going to turn me into a chicken?" The answer is of course not, silly. But secretly, I can turn anybody into a chicken. And, so can you.

Don't worry, you won't need to hypnotize anyone. A little mind-control will suffice. Moreover, the mind you'll control will be your own. This is perfectly safe, only it does require a sense of humor. You're going to train your brain to remain undisturbed—indeed, even pleasantly amused—by the boor's presence, regardless of their annoying antics, in order to protect your leadership mojo.

But first, a little behind-the-scenes neuroscience. You're about to harness the substantial power of your visual cortex through using mental imagery. With the repetition of practice, you'll create new long-term brain-cell connections, training your subconscious to conjure up a particular picture whenever you encounter the problem person. That, in turn, will influence two emotional regulators, your insular cortex and your amygdala, so that your subconscious brain will bypass annoyance and go straight to amusement.

Now you know why it works. Ready? Just follow these easy steps:

How to Turn People into Chickens

1. Treat yourself to a comfy chair in a quiet place where you can close your eyes for a minute or two.

2. Close your eyes and take a moment to get relaxed—belly breathing, perhaps?

3. Bring into your imagination, as best you can, an image of Negative Nelly or Ned. For now, let this be a silent flic, so put them on mute. Make the picture as vivid and lifelike as possible in your mind's eye.

4. Now put them in a chicken suit. In all seriousness—create an image that's so absurd you make yourself smile. Watch them strut, sit, gesture, fluff their feathers, whatever.

5. (Optional) If you want, add audio and let them talk. Then change their voice to a comical squawking. However, be careful, because if you actually need to hear what they say— for example, if they're your CEO or your accountant—then it's safer to just do visuals.

6. Practice enjoying this mind-movie clip several times a day for a week or more. This will create long-lasting connections in your brain's neural circuitry.

7. Whenever you encounter the offender in person, as best you can, "see" them in their chicken suit. You may need to consciously remind yourself at times, but the more you practice (alone and in their company), the more your subconscious will automatically generate the effect when

they're present. Of course, you'll continue to accurately discern their real-life appearance—don't worry, you're not going to hallucinate—but now at some level of your consciousness, they'll be tucked into a chicken suit. Enjoy!

Please only use this tactic when appropriate, and never on friends, family, or intimates, because there is one side effect. By defusing the person's negative impact, you'll begin to find that individual pathetic and truly pitiful. However, there's no need to feel unkind about it, because in the long run, you might be doing them a favor. It's possible they'll eventually register that their negative antics no longer get a rise out of you. This could catalyze a shift toward the positive. Someday that chicken may cross that road—and only *you* will know why.

It's a Wrap!

So, there you have it, a new set of mind-bending—as in brain-plasticizing—strategies to oust subconscious saboteurs from your workplace. Here's a recap to take with you:

1. **Eradicate the what-the-hell effect.** To restore willpower and motivation, replace shame with forgiveness (keeping in mind that all humans make mistakes).

2. **Finish off the fixed mindset.** To re-ignite your people's confidence, courage, and creativity—not to mention work ethic!—stop praising anyone for talent or smarts. Instead, applaud their effort and share the good news of neuroplasticity.

3. **Negate the negative.** Sometimes there's that one malcontent who seems to want nothing more than to ruin your life. Although anyone can change, you can't change everyone. So, you've got to know when and how to play chicken.

For research citations and fun free stuff including a mini-course on self-hypnosis, come visit self-intelligence.com. And if you've taught your dog how to fold your laundry or to put on socks, please send your video to jane@janeransom.com. May the subconscious force be with you.

Jane Ransom is an international brain-trainer, habit-changer, master hypnotist and recognized expert on the subconscious mind. The London-based publisher Quarto Group has released worldwide her book *Self-Intelligence: The New Science-Based Approach for Reaching Your True Potential.* A former journalist and professor, Jane now pairs her communication skills with her passion to serve the world. Over the last decade she has led many hundreds of clients to bust through inner gridlock by using her neuroplasticity-driven model of Self-Intelligence®.

She helps individuals transform their lives and works with organizations to improve leadership, employee engagement, creativity, and healthy habits. Jane's enthusiasm for brain science might have turned her into an eccentric autodidact, if not for the mentorship of Jack Canfield, who taught Jane how to tell people to get off their butts—but in a really nice way.

A native mid-westerner, Jane also has lived in New York, Boston, Madrid, Paris, San Juan (Puerto Rico), and San Francisco. In San

Francisco, she conducted her hypnosis-coaching practice out of the historic Phelan Building. Recently, she relocated to Durham, North Carolina, a thriving hub of cutting-edge research. To learn more about her Self-Intelligence® speaking and training services, please visit janeransom.com

Section Three
Leading Organizations

CHAPTER 9

Leading Change
How to Create True, Meaningful, and Impactful Change in Your Organization

by Amina Makhdoom

When people ask me what I do, I say I am in the business of changing people. This is always a great conversation starter, because smart people know that you cannot change someone else. So, it piques their curiosity on how exactly I do this near impossible task. More importantly, they are curious how I have built a business and reputation around this.

In my sixteen years as a Management Consultant, I have seen all types of business initiatives from automation, to reducing costs, to innovation projects, and while each of the projects are unique in their own way, and have completely different models to get the return on investment (ROI), they all have one common, huge, hurdle: they involve people changing their behavior. Over the years, I have found that this one hurdle can make or break the project and can cause companies to either obtain or lose their ROI.

Yet, each time I am called into a company—usually when they are already in crisis mode, halfway through the project—and I talk about the solution that is to help people navigate change, there is so much resistance. Earlier in my career, I used to get frustrated about this, but now I have realized this comes from a deep sense of hopelessness by leadership on how to actually get people to change in a way that is self-motivated and not top-down imposed.

However, I have discovered proven strategies that result in internally motivated change within a company. Once applied, I have seen these strategies work time and time again. They are straight forward and simple, but not easy to apply. I have found that one of the greatest challenges to this is that change causes people to think poorly of their leadership. Leaders, who genuinely want what is best for not only the company and bottom line, but also their people, become defensive and demotivated by this negative perception. There is a gap here and the gap is in perception, not in reality. I begin by creating an understanding of how these perceptions occur and then move to the specific steps that leaders, at all levels of the organization, can take to ensure perception stays on their side and how they can support the creation of True Change—one that is motivated from the inside and expressed in the business place leading to the business results all hope to achieve.

Change is Hard, but How Did It Make Me into the Company Monster?

Does this sound familiar to you? You, or your organization, have invested x million dollars on the project that will transform your business. An external company came in and made their presentation. You were there, everything they said made sense, and it sounded like the answers to your wishes. Now, you are x number of months/years into the project and all these "issues" have popped up. When you go back to the external company, they tell you that it turns out you are not the "simple" client that can have this solution applied in the simplest way, but there are a number of business and personnel issues that have to be cleaned up before you will ever see any return of investment on this project. The fine print states that it would be your job to ensure your processes and people fit the new technology.

You seem to remember hearing that and thinking, "I'm sure they will. This makes so much sense. How could it not?" Now, you are in the position where you have to decide if you're going to continue to invest money in this project and hope that the company and people can change enough to get the ROI, or if you're going to cut your losses and go back to how you used to do things, while looking for another more aptly suited solution that will fit within the budget you now have remaining.

I have seen this scenario too many times to count. If you have been in this situation, you are not alone. If you have experienced it, I totally sympathize. This is usually where someone realizes what they really need is some good business process design and change management—the Hail Mary of project management. By this time in most projects, it is too late. You are already looking at more investment of time and money to get the results you originally wanted. Both the project leaders, as well as people like me (the change management consultants), wish they had made the call earlier so more time could have been spent up front on the people and process that would have resulted in a backend saving of time, money, and frustration.

During these large-scale changes, organizations lose some of their best employees. These are the people that put their heart and soul into the sinking project and are now exhausted, demotivated, and disenchanted. If or when the project is saved, it is implemented with less than optimal results. Many times, the project is implemented for egotistical reasons with results that may hurt the organization in the long term, and that definitely hurt the reputation of the leader.

Given my background in organizational and human performance, I knew there had to be a better way. I would go to project after project and see millions of dollars spent on something that I knew from the first day would not work, because the upfront work was faulty or incomplete. It was so obvious to me, that I assumed it was obvious to others. It was not until this happened a few times that I realized I tended to say the same things over and over again, gave the same advice, and took the same actions to save these failing projects. Based on years of experience on saving projects by building up people to do what it takes to be successful, I have learned the key actions that every organization must follow to successfully implement change.

The Biggest Hurdle—You don't know, and they aren't telling you... at least not in a way you can understand.

My first introduction to getting people to change came at the age of six, when one of my friends got into trouble for something she did not do. She sat there and took the blame as her mother berated her for something that we both knew another child had done. At that age, I had no concept of boundaries, privacy, or social constructs, but I sure did have a good understanding of right and wrong. I marched up to her mother, in the middle of her lecture, boldly interrupted, and told her how she was completely wrong, how she did not have the whole story, and how she really needed to apologize to her daughter for her poor behavior. As cute as this may sound now, my friend's mother was not amused by my confrontation. Not only did she not apologize to her daughter, but she went to my mother in an attempt to get me in trouble and informed her how I had been rude and talked back.

There are two lessons from this story based on what happened next. First of all, my mother, who was all about social graces, immediately sought me out, but instead of yelling at me, she asked me what happened (probably because she could see that I was still seething and was afraid I would tell her off next). After all, a wrong had occurred, and it had not yet been made right. After I passionately (with only the necessary amount of drama) explained about the crime against humanity, I was only more worked up—this time at my friend for not speaking up. Why was I the only one who cared? Justice had to be served. How did my friend not see that?

Unfortunately, at the time, that meant yelling at my friend for "allowing" her mother to treat her that way. I could not fathom how my friend sat there and took the blame for something that she clearly did not do. Mind you, my friend was not happy about getting in trouble by her mother, but she was by no means traumatized by this event; she just did not really care. She had learned that it did not matter if she spoke up; her mother was going to blow up anyway. She would survive and move on.

What I saw then, and still see today, is that there is no learning and growth when we do not speak up and share our perspective. I learned something big that day: when people are in the presence of power, they often do not speak their truth because they think it will not matter anyway. In companies, I see this every day. "Well, they made the decision. They are not going to want to hear from me how it will not work. I will be known as a naysayer." Employees are ok with letting a situation go unresolved or misinformation to rule rather than risk speaking up (to executives) and dealing with any personal inconvenience to do so. But that lesson shows how leaders and organizations mature with experience and how the first big change project is always worse than the tenth big change project. By the tenth project, leaders have painfully learned the lesson and do not need to rely as heavily on their employees to tell them.

But, imagine you knew ahead of time where your company's land mines were and could plan for them before starting the project. This is one of the main reasons that organizations hire me. They have amazing leaders—ones who care about their employees, who want to listen, who are open to hearing what is and is not working, yet these leaders rarely hear the impeccable, microscopic truth from their employees. This microscopic truth—these unsaid ideas—could save the organization millions of dollars and tons of time, but they either never get heard, are stopped somewhere up the chain of command to the leader, or worse, are proposed by someone who has a reputation as a "troublemaker" or lacks communication skills, so they are not well-received even when they are being told.

At this point, it would be easy to pontificate the five things you could do as a leader, or the ten mistakes leaders make, etc. But with my background in Change Management, I realize it is not the five or ten behaviors, but something deeper; it is the heart and authenticity of the leader that make those behaviors automatic and welcome or contrived and failing. That is what True Change is. It is not about an action, but a way of being, that allows True Change to find its way into your organization. The good news is that this change is something that you can do without buying anything or investing in some large-scale program. It involves changing your perspective and catching yourself when you are out of a heart-centered place.

Now, either you are feeling really good about yourself, because you perceive yourself as heart-centered and authentic, or you are starting to get worried that you are going to have to do "touchy-feely" stuff to implement a new computer system. Remember that every single skill you have, whether you perceive it as good or bad, has a positive and negative element to it. So, let's get real and see where you fall on the Heart Centered Leadership Discovery Scale.

1. What percentage of your time do you spend in "reality," and what percentage of your time do you spend in "possibility"?

2. Do you believe that every person you interact with has value and something to teach you, if you are willing and open to learn? Every single one, like the homeless woman on the side of the street asking for money to Warren Buffet? When you make decisions, what part do you base on analytical results (facts and figures), and what part do you base on intuition and inner knowing? Have you ever walked away from an

amazing opportunity because it did not *feel* right?

3. At the end of the day, what is your organization about? Bottom line? Making a profit? Supporting the community? Creating a new innovative product, idea, or culture? What do you want to achieve at the macro level with your company? How does this show up in how your organization works?

The answers to these questions will lead you to understand which of the three areas below may need your attention. In order for True Change to occur within organizations, you need to understand your real process—why your people really come to work—and then elevate yourself to come from a place of true heart to drive the change. If you pick up any book on leadership, corporate culture, or organizational behavior, every single one of them will dedicate a section on clarity of goals/direction and constant communication. For that reason, I am going to skip both of those, but with the agreement and understanding, both items are critical for any kind of organizational and employee success. What are the key principles that make large-scale change efforts successful?

> *True Change is not about an action, but about a way of being.*

I. Process – How does your business really run? Understanding the actual business process, not the ideal business process, is vital.

Do you know how your business really runs? Most people in executive leadership do not. Most leaders know the policies, procedures, and process flows, but they are amazed (not in a good way) when they find out what is actually going on in the organization to get the work done. I think many don't know because it would be depressing if they actually saw it. The exception may be manufacturing environments where the process is highly automated, but even in those environments, there is a ton of waste and many opportunities for improvement.

A big part of the reason that leaders don't know what is really happening is because when they walk the floor, people stand a little taller, work a little cleaner, and act like there are no issues. Those that don't are often labeled troublemakers or face the potential for some form of retaliation from their immediate supervisor. The *make your boss look good* attitude leads to covering up inefficient processes and real problems. Remember the example of my friend when I was a child? There is a general feeling that speaking up, telling the microscopic level of truth, is a career-limiting move.

Here is an example from a large, high tech, cutting edge medical device company, where employees were being compensated very well for their job. This example is from a process interview prior to implementing a new system. One of the necessities in every environment I work in is to "walk the floor" and talk to people to see what is *really* happening.

Me: Ok, so they complete the form and email it to you, then what happens?

Pat: Then, I print the form out, review it, and I walk it over to Barbara's desk on the second floor.

Me: Ok, what do you review the form for?

Pat: Just to make sure it is not blank. I make sure it looks like everything is filled out.

Me: Ok, once you give it to Barbara, what does she do with it?

Pat: I'm not sure. I think she has to enter the information from the form into her system.

Me: Doesn't the original form come from the same system? Isn't the information already in there?

Pat: Yeah, I guess so. But I still need to do my final check.

Me: Couldn't you just email the form directly to Barbara? You know, it would save you the walk (my attempt to be cute).

Pat: Well, that is the only time of the day I see Barbara. And normally, when I bring her any forms, we get to catch up, and we usually walk to the break area and get coffee.

Me: That sounds like fun. You must get along well with Barbara?

Pat: I do. It is the best part of my day.

Me: Thanks for your time. I am just a little confused about one thing that I'm hoping you can help me understand. The person sends you the form; you review it, then print it, and take it to Barbara. What would happen if the person filled out the form directly in the system? Would they just let Barbara know they did it, and she can pull it up? Would that work?

Pat: I suppose so, but who would print it?

Me: Does it need to be printed if it is in the system?

Pat: I'm not sure, but I think Barbara likes when it is printed out.

Me: Ok, that makes sense. Thanks for talking to me about this. I think I will meet with Barbara too and understand what she does. Let me know if you think of anything else that may be helpful.

When I tell this story, or the hundreds of others like it, many leaders laugh and shake their heads in judgment of Pat and Barbara. But we all are just like Pat and Barbara. We all have a way we like to do things for our own personal reasons. If you do not account for this in your organization, you are setting up the organization to create inefficiencies. Read that again. Without getting real about how things are happening, you create a process that your company cannot sustain, and this eventually leads to the change failing. So how do you handle this situation?

The first thing I told Pat and Barbara when we were implementing a new process was that it does not need to impact their coffee ritual—they can continue to do that, but without a printed form. If the organization does not allow for this, what you would get instead is *resistance to change* where the same system remains in place, and Pat is still printing out the form and walking it to Barbara. In addition, since this is a change, you also have to determine how the new process provides enough "good" things for people to fully embrace and accept it. I did find out that they used to have issues with people using the wrong cost center, and Pat's check was created years ago (pre-Pat) to ensure the cost center was accurate before it went to Barbara. But since the cost centers had become so commonplace in the company, the cost center check had not been needed for many years.

Yet the process remained. The person before Pat printed out the form, checked the cost center, and walked it down to Barbara. Without spending time sitting with Pat and Barbara at their desks, watching their movements, and asking why they do what they do, I would not have found this issue. Group interviews with tons of employees talking about your high-level process will not tell you where you are going to fail with a new system/process or change effort.

2. People – Why do your employees really come to work each day?

Do you know why your employees wake up, dress, and drive the 10-, 30-, 45-minute or 2-hour commute every day to come to work? For most people, it is not because they believe in the mission, vision, and values of your organization—although if they did not, they would not continue to come. Something else motivates them to keep coming, to not call in sick as often as possible, or find another reason to not be there. For the majority of them, it is their personal relationships. Your employees show up much more for each other than they do for you. They show up to have coffee with their friend in the next cubicle, have lunch with the guys, escape mommy-mode for eight solid hours, or to bury themselves in something that uses a skill set they enjoy using. Very few employees show up to work for the mission of the job. But most employees stay and weather the hard times (missed promotions, no raises, bad supervisors) for the mission of the company. Mission, vision, and values are important, but to get an internally motivated employee, it is not enough.

There are two types of motivation that lead to what I call an internally motivated employee: intrinsic and extrinsic motivation. Here is where it gets complicated because we have two words that imply internal. Let's break it down. There are two types of motivation: internal and external. External motivation is great, but it is hard, time consuming, expensive, and only works on some employees, some of the time, and with short term results. This is what all the business motivation books are about. While external motivation is not going to get your company where it needs to be, without it, organizations would be completely dysfunctional. So, you need external motivation. Examples of these include a paycheck, recognition, employee wellness programs, etc.

Then there is internal motivation. This is free, easy, works on most employees, and works most of the time. This is the kind of motivation you want in your company—people who come to work internally motivated to do a good job. It is not dependent on your employee initiative *du jour*. Within this internally motivated employee, there are two types of processes to motivate. Some processes are intrinsic, meaning you are speaking to how employees view themselves. Other processes are extrinsic, meaning you are speaking to how employees perceive how others view them and/or how they want to be viewed by others. People do things because they believe a) they will be a better person if they do it, or b) others will think they are a better person if they do it. Both of these are powerful tools that each person uses to govern themselves with, and therefore powerful tools to address when creating change.

In my years of experience, I have met numerous employees who were willing to be in a little more pain so that their colleague—who was in a lot of pain—would be in less pain; this is the concept of taking one for the team. They were willing to make their own life a little harder so that someone else's life was a little easier. This is extrinsic motivation at its best. You see this example all the time among siblings, for example, an older sibling doing their homework to set a good example for the younger sibling. This is part of the reason that teams are so successful. Team members are pulling their weight to help the other members of the team. When you have high-performing teams, you see team members really show up and be there for one another.

In order to have internally motivated employees, you have to understand what is important to them. This may sound like a daunting task, but it does not have to be. I suggest that leaders make time on their calendar to have five conversations a week with their employees. Choose five of your employees each week and get to know them a bit. This does not need to take more than ten minutes each. By dedicating an hour a week to your employees, you will start to see, very quickly, why they come to work and while at work, whom they are motivated to help. Knowing your employees on a personal level is just as important as knowing your business strategy. Think of your employees as the vehicle that is going to get you to your strategic goal—you want to know the ins and outs of how that vehicle works. This includes the pesky situations that may come up that would cause a full vehicular breakdown. Only by knowing the people who are going to get you to the finish line will you be able to learn how to best plan to meet your strategic objectives.

3. Heart Centered Approach – Understanding that value is everywhere... your job is to find it!

Do you really understand how to find the value in your organization? Everyone who is working in your organization today is bringing some form of value to the table. Are you honing your skills to see what the value is? Are you able to distinguish if this is the value you need right now? Are you strong enough to remove those people whose value is not a current fit for your organization? Each person is adding something to your company (your life) every day, and it is your job to determine if what they are adding is useful or not. There are some well-known quotes and statistics that say you are the average of the five people you spend the most time with, and your environment dictates more of your behavior than anything else.

I have worked in a number of organizations, each with their own corporate culture. It takes only a few minutes at a company to begin to pick up the corporate culture, and less than a week to understand the stated and "real" corporate culture. When an organization is about the bottom line and making a profit, you can feel it when you walk in the door. When the organization is about teamwork and customer service, you can feel that when you walk in the door. It takes moments to *feel* what the culture of your organization is all about. When I meet the leaders, it only takes a few minutes longer to see how the organization got the type of culture it has. Are you clear about why your organization exists? Are you happy with why your organization exists? Is it possible that you actually have the perfect people in place for why your organization exists, even the ones that you like the least? Your organization and its culture attract a specific type of person. If you feel like your employees are [fill in the blank], then look at what your organization is about and see if it is actually supporting that.

The people who annoy and bother you the most, usually have the most to teach you. There comes a time when it is best to part ways, but not before you learn the lesson. Each person with whom you interact is there to help you with your own growth and development. The ones you want to run the furthest from the fastest, unfortunately, usually have the most to teach you. Think of someone in your organization today that really bothers you. Now ask yourself, in what ways am I like this person? Really sit with that question. My guess is that you have found hundreds of ways that you are different, but the learning comes in seeing how you are the same.

The learning comes in seeing how this person may be reflecting all of your worst qualities that you would rather not look at. Identify what those qualities are; realize that the mirror was a gift to see how those qualities may come across to others. This person, just like you, may have great intentions, but some rough edges. Once you see that this is just another person, with good and bad points, ask yourself critically if they fit into the organization you have created and if they add value to the organization in a positive way. That will tell you if they belong in your organization or if it is time to help them find a better fit for the value they provide.

> *To change, you have to raise your level of awareness. The more aware you are, the easier it is to change.*

Take a few minutes now to think of someone who really bothers you. Make a list of the things about them that you do not like. Now, look at that list and ask yourself if you display any of those behaviors as well.

Change is hard because our minds are so amazing. They have gotten so used to doing things in a certain way, that they go on autopilot. To change, you have to raise your level of awareness. The more aware you are, the easier it is to change. The more you live a life on autopilot, the harder it is to change. Most organizations know that change is how they improve and get to the next level, rise to their competitors' challenge, and innovate to create new and exciting offerings. This is not easy to remember in each moment, and there may be times that you forget it's a habit and a muscle that can be developed like any other. By clearly identifying one action step you will take, and measuring it regularly, you may be amazed to see how much change occurs in a matter of months.

In order for True Change, you have to commit to truly changing. The information in this chapter is not complicated, but the process—of being more open, seeing value in every situation, allowing space for people to tell the microscopic truth about how work is done—is not easy. It is simple, but simple does not mean easy. Decide today to walk around your organization and identify the value that each person is bringing to the table. Decide to ask yourself how the person who annoys you the most, is the most like you; what qualities of your own do you see in them?

By remembering that change includes people, process, and technology (not just technology with the hopes that people and process will catch up to it one day), you can make change a personal and professional growth opportunity for you and your organization using Heart-Centered Leadership, resulting in True Change. My hope is that this results not only in greater ROI, but also happier, healthier, more productive relationships and workforces, leading to innovative ideas that support the growth of your organization.

Amina Makhdoom's background in corporate America combined with her extensive training in human potential allows her to deliver cutting-edge information in a manner that resonates clearly with business audiences. Her mission is to leave you with a clear objective, tangible actions to reach the next step and inspiration and personal realization of your own power. She focuses more on helping you reveal within yourself your own ability to achieve extraordinary results. Amina is affectionately labeled *A Ray of Sunshine,* not only for her positive attitude and disposition, but for her warmth and ability to connect with each person in the room creating a space that allows for growth. For more on Amina's work, visit: askamina.com and lunchwithcinderella.com

CHAPTER 10

Planning with Passion
Business Strategizing for Inspired Leaders

by Connie Whitesell, CPC, MBA

Are you feeling it may be time to take your business planning from a "should do" to an "inspired done"? The Planning with Passion system combines the most effective traditional business planning methods with empowering inspirational and accountability techniques to lead you through a step-by-step plan of action that revs you up and takes you to exactly where you want to be—and better.

I established my management consulting business in 2000 with a human-resources focus. My mission was to help organizations and their leaders understand how to treat their employees well and to understand the myriad of complex federal, state, and local employment laws. It was interesting to me, though, how often the topics of strategic planning kept arising. Luckily, I received the greatest pleasure and most professional success from helping my clients do their planning. As a result, I expanded the business into business and strategic planning and professional coaching in 2011.

At the same time, on the personal development side, I had been incorporating the power of spiritual practices and inner work, using visualization, affirmations, and meditations to create miracles in my personal life. I had rarely seen these processes of business planning and spiritual development combined. Think about it. We can possess the clarity that comes with getting all of those brilliant ideas down on paper and organized, while at the same time, making a deeper connection with our highest inner being to gain even more powerful insight and guidance into our business.

I had been planning in my own business for years, but once I combined these processes and techniques, my work took off—skyrocketed in ways I never could have imagined. Speaking opportunities, long-term client contracts, and collaboration opportunities with other coaches and change leaders became a regular occurrence. In 2014, I created a new business, Scattered to Streamlined Business Coaching, devoted entirely to helping small business owners create the work of their dreams.

Just as exciting was seeing similar changes happen in my clients' businesses. One, a fashion consultant who initially worked with individuals, expanded her offerings so that now she works with companies who help their managers present themselves more professionally. Another, a musician, was inspired through our work together to create a gospel-themed brunch. He now is creating a movie score. Another HVAC business owner went from doing time-consuming residential work to highly successful commercial projects. The day I wrote this paragraph, he informed me that he signed a contract to work with ninety franchises of a well-known Mexican fast-food chain.

It really does not matter what the industry is. What matters is the passion that goes into the planning.

The Planning with Passion process incorporates three main elements:

1. *Traditional Business Planning Elements.* Look at the core categories of your business and take time to consider what you want for the future of your work. Develop powerful objectives, strategies, and action plans. With these, you will know exactly what you need to do on a quarterly or monthly basis, or from week to week and day to day to keep moving forward toward your final vision.

2. *Empowering Inspirational Techniques.* While the traditional business planning elements are critical to your plan, so is allowing for flexibility. Most importantly though, is allowing time and space for inspiration. For this reason, incorporate tools that are not often taught to students in business school: affirmations, visualization methods, and just plain finding time for quiet contemplation. These techniques are critical to helping get that inspiration and flow of great energy behind everything you do, including your business development efforts.

3. *Good Sense Business Elements*
   - *Taking Action.* An African proverb states: "When you pray, move your feet." No amount of planning, meditating, or saying affirmations is going to get you anywhere if you never leave your computer or meditation pillow and simply wait for something to happen.

- *Accountability.* Share with others your plans and allow them to provide support to you, even if it's just moral support. This makes a huge difference in whether you take the action you say you will.

- *Frequent Plan Review and Revision.* Once you are finished with your plan, the worst thing is to stick it in a drawer and never look at it again. That is a surefire way to ensure you will end up in the same place next year that you are in right now.

The Planning with Passion system is a fluid, ever-changing one—an ongoing process of celebrating accomplishments, acknowledging and overcoming challenges, and shifting plans and strategies as unexpected opportunities keep coming your way. It is the interaction of these three elements that makes this process so effective. That is Planning with Passion in a nutshell.

Now, let's dig a little deeper!

THE VISION FOR YOUR WORK

Be brave, be fierce, be visionary. Mend the parts of the world that are 'within your reach.' To live this way is the most dramatic gift you can ever give to the world. Consider yourselves assigned.

– American Poet, Clarissa Pinkola Estes

When was the last time you took just a few minutes of quiet, focused time to close your eyes and simply sit in contemplation of what the ideal vision of your work (or your life, for that matter) looks like?

Find a quiet space where you will not be interrupted. Sit comfortably, close your eyes, allow your mind to float away and allow yourself to envision your work in its fullest expression of success in the next year and beyond. Let anything that comes to mind reside there without judgment. When you feel complete with the vision, gradually allow yourself to return to awareness of your current surroundings, open your eyes, and jot down notes of everything that came to you. Nothing is too miniscule or unimportant.

If doing this without a guide is a struggle, review the following list of questions first, then follow the process explained above. It may even be helpful to record yourself slowly reading the questions out loud, then listening to the recording while sitting in contemplation.

When I introduce this visioning process to my clients, I sometimes hear remarks about it seeming a bit unusual or "out there," usually followed by an uncomfortable giggle. If you experience a similar feeling, be open to trying this just once. Taking the time to allow yourself to create the inner vision for your work, to see it in your mind and feel what it is like to achieve your objectives, has such power—both in guiding you to determining your vision and in supporting the achievement of your goals.

Questions for Consideration:

- Who are you working with? What is your ideal client like?
- Where are you working? In an office, out of your home, primarily traveling to clients, or a combination of these?

- What are the services and/or products that you most enjoy developing and providing that your clients are most welcome to receiving?

- How are you letting potential clients know about all of the wonderful services and/or products you have to offer? Are you speaking to people directly—in person, by phone, or group settings, such as educational events? Are you connecting more with people electronically, through email, social media, online classes? Feel yourself making those connections in an authentic and effective way.

- How are people working in your business interacting with each other in your ideal vision?

- What does your ideal workweek look like? How about your ideal workday?

- What is your ideal monthly or annual income?

- How are you expressing your unique gifts in your work?

- What else do you think about when you envision your ideal business experience?

Be sure to take notes of everything that came to you in your vision. Repeat this exercise every day as you work on your business planning. New ideas will arise as you go deeper into past visions for your work.

The Roadmap to Success

Business planning, in an overall sense, can be overwhelming. There are so many aspects to consider and so many ideas to flesh out and implement. I've made this process easier by "chunking" things down into four fundamental categories that most businesses share:

- Services and/or Products
- Operations
- Marketing and Sales
- Finances

Certain sections require more attention than others. While each may be tweaked in some way toward improvement in your work, focus the majority of your time on the sections that are *critical* to your business or work. If one of these areas is fine, skip that section.

Key Category: Services and Products

In this section, it is important not only to describe what you are selling or providing, but also to evaluate its quality, packaging, pricing, delivery, and research and development aspects.

What do you offer?

Before you begin your analysis for this category, take a few moments to create a list of all of the services and products you offer. For each service or product, consider and describe:

- A summary of the service/product
- Its key features
- The problem it solves for your client
- The way it is packaged and/or provided
- Its cost
- Its uniqueness in comparison to your competitors' offerings

- Anything else important to know about this service/product

Analysis of services and/or products

The following is a set of general questions that relate to this category for most businesses. Read through this list and jot down notes with whatever thoughts come to you. Again, if some questions do not apply, skip them. You likely will think of other statements that pertain to this category. Go ahead and add them as you see fit.

Quality and quantity

- Is the quality of your services and products at its highest level?

- Do your services and products have something about them that makes them unique?

- Are your services and products well-defined and relevant to your target market?

- Do they deliver clear value to your clients?

- Do you offer a comprehensive set of services and products to address all client needs in your business area?

- Do you plan on adding services/products in the future?

- Do you offer services and products that should be eliminated from your offerings due to lack of desirability or obsolescence?

Packaging

- Are your services and products packaged in a way that will best appeal to your customers?

- Can they be repackaged or tailored to individual client needs?

Pricing/fees

- Do you have an effective pricing/fee strategy? (i.e. high-end, middle of the road, low-cost)
- Does your pricing/fee strategy compare well with your competitors?
- Is your pricing/fee strategy sufficient to cover your costs, plus a profit margin?
- Do you offer a range of payment options?
- Have you adjusted your prices/fees as the experience and quality of your services and products have improved?

Delivery

- Do your delivery systems operate effectively?
- Are you providing timely services/support to your clients?

Research and development

- Do you have systems in place to ensure you keep up-to-date on regulatory requirements, trends, tools, and/or technologies affecting your business?
- Do you develop new offerings or enhance current ones to ensure your services and products are up-to-date and relevant?

Rating of success

After giving these questions consideration, on a scale of 1-10, how you would rate your business currently in terms of its expression of success? For example, a rating of "1" would indicate that your services and products are nowhere near your fullest expression of success. They are not anywhere near how you envision them being. A rating of "10" would indicate the fullest expression of success.

Your products and services are just the way you want them and just the way your clients love them.

Write that rating down. There are no wrong or right answers. This number simply gives you a benchmark. A low number means you have many opportunities to play within this category. A higher number means you can be more focused.

Key objectives

Based on your consideration of the various elements of the services and product categories, and your rating of success, develop a list of your key objectives. These objective statements will respond to the question: What do I need to do with my services and products to get my business closer to a rating of "10"?

Strategies and action steps

Refer to the planning sheet following this section. Feel free to use this format, or something similar, to work through your detailed planning. To begin, select your most important objective from this category, and write it at the top of the page. Now drill down, and keep getting more specific as you develop strategies and steps for taking action.

Many people have a tendency to avoid doing things that make them uncomfortable or provide too much of a challenge outside of their comfort zones. The planning sheet section with "challenges/weaknesses" allows you to think through any external challenges or internal weaknesses your business has with relation to this objective.

Example #1: Terry wants to expand his marketing consulting services into conducting in-person workshops, knowing that they will be invaluable to his business development. The problem is that he does not yet feel comfortable speaking in front of groups. Terry contemplated this challenge and came up with a few ideas for solutions. These solutions became a part of his strategies. He was able to further identify specific action steps that flowed from these strategies.

Sample Objective #1: Deliver motivational workshops to professional associations on at least a quarterly basis throughout the calendar year.

Sample Strategy #1: Become comfortable speaking live before groups of people.

Sample Action Steps

- Find and join a local Toastmasters group. Due date: January 30th
- Actively participate in Toastmasters at least once per month. (February through December)
- Find and hire a speaking coach. Due date: February 15th

Likewise, consider your external opportunities and internal strengths, and determine ways you may take advantage of opportunities and make the most of and/or maintain your business strengths. More strategies will develop, as in the following continuation of the previous example.

Sample Strategy #2: Research speaking opportunities in my local area.

Sample Action Steps

- Discuss potential opportunities with representatives of my local professional business development group. (List representatives and groups.) Due date: March 1st
- Inform corporate clients of this additional service. (Sub-action steps: list clients and dates by which you will contact them.)

When you have completed the analysis of your initial objective, continue the process with your remaining ones.

Inspirational Element: Affirmations

In the planning worksheet template, there is a section for creating an affirmation for your objective. An affirmation is a statement that describes a goal as if it is already achieved. I want you to feel amazing when you think about obtaining this objective.

Affirmations work!

- They hold a vision of what you know can be true.
- They shift perspective from limiting thoughts to positive beliefs.
- They stress the importance of achieving your objective to your subconscious so it begins working for you, noticing opportunities to take you closer to your goal.

Suggestions for creating an affirmation:

- Begin with "I am" or "I feel"
- State the feeling of having achieved the goal

- Use present tense
- Include an action word

Examples:
- "I feel so fulfilled to now be sharing my knowledge and providing valuable insights to my clients in a warm and welcoming group setting."
- "I am jumping for joy, having completed my book and am now sharing it with the world."
- "I am ecstatic to have signed a multiyear contract with my first corporate client and am enthusiastically preparing a program tailored perfectly to their needs."

Tips for using affirmations:
- Repeat it out loud, if possible, every time you review your objective.
- Keep repeating the affirmation until you deeply feel the emotion behind the affirmation.

Now create that powerful affirming statement of having achieved your goal. Say it with emotion. Feel it from your heart.

PLANNING WORKSHEET

Objective #___:

Challenge/Weakness	
Solution	
Opportunity/Strength	
Make most of	

Strategy #1

Action Step	Due Date	Persons Involved
1.		
2.		
3.		

Strategy #2

Action Step	Due Date	Persons Involved
1.		
2.		
3.		

Strategy #3

Action Step	Due Date	Persons Involved
1.		
2.		
3.		

Affirmation:

_____

_____

_____

Key Category: Operations

In this section, consider whether you have the resources and systems in place that are necessary to produce, and provide the highest quality of services and products in the most efficient manner.

Follow the same steps outlined in the Services and Products section, for the Analysis of Operations category utilizing the questions provided below:

1. Determine your 1-10 success rating
2. Develop your key objectives
3. Outline your strategies and action steps

Questions to consider:

Business structure

- Is your business structured legally in the most beneficial way, given your present situation and your vision for your work?
- Have you assessed certifications and related opportunities available to small businesses and businesses owned by women, minorities, or disabled persons, if applicable?

Technology resources

Do you have technological systems in place to support your business from both an administrative and client support perspective? Are you utilizing them to their fullest potential?

- Website capabilities
- Electronic communications systems
- General and industry-specific software/hardware

Human resources

Do you have the internal and external support you require to effectively service your clients? Are you utilizing these human resources to their fullest potential?

- Administrative
- Sales/Marketing
- Customer Service
- Legal
- Financial
- Employee Relations
- Information Technology
- Production

Systems

Are your business processes clearly identified, documented, and implemented?

- Billing
- Contracts
- Scheduling
- Sales/Marketing
- Customer Service
- Financial Reporting
- If you have employees, are policies and procedures developed and effectively communicated?

Physical space

- Do you have sufficient and comfortable space to conduct your work?

- Is your business space conducive to your business practices?

Inspiratonal Element: Visual Tools

As I developed this system, I found myself craving visual tools to enhance the program. Here are some of my favorites that I implement on a regular basis:

1. A Planning Binder

   Keep your plan in a 3-ring binder divided by sections according to each business category. Put your planning worksheets in chronological order or in order of importance. As you accomplish each objective, put a satisfying note of completion across the front of the sheet.

2. Photos and Pictures

   The Internet makes it easy to find pictures and photos that represent your various professional goals and objectives. Simply use the "images" feature of any search engine. Once you find an image that speaks to your heart, copy and paste it onto your planning worksheet. This pop of color and visual reminder of the objective you want to achieve, will warm your heart any time you look at your plan.

   Add the most fabulous picture to the cover of your planning binder.

3. Vision Board for Business

   I have never been a "vision board" kind of gal. I always

found them difficult to create until I developed the following process.

Planning with Passion—Vision Board Process

Supplies

- One framed bulletin board (more attractive and long-lasting than cardboard and easily obtainable from any office supply store)
- A set of attractive thumbtacks (more versatile than tape or glue)
- Scissors
- A computer with Internet access
- A color printer loaded with high-quality paper

Process

- Review your plan and objectives and determine which of them may be easily represented with a photo, drawing, or image.

Perhaps you have a vision in your mind of your ideal client. Search the Internet for photos that match the various characteristics of that individual.

Maybe you wish to begin or expand your public speaking practice. Find a photo of one of your favorite speakers presenting before a group. If you have the capability, you can Photoshop your face onto the photo. Perhaps a large red photo of "TED" would be perfect in representing a goal of giving a TED or a TEDx talk.

If the ability to work from anywhere is your goal, and you have a special love for the water, find a photo of someone working on their laptop at a table with an umbrella facing the ocean.

Find appropriate photos/drawings/pictures online, print them, and cut to size.

- Attach the photos to the bulletin board. Move them around until you are happy with the collage.

- Put your vision board in a place where you will see it every day. Not only do I have my vision board in my office, but I also have a photo of it saved as the opening photo on my cell phone. I can't get away from my dreams if I tried!

4. A Vision Movie

   Create your own vision movie using your favorite presentation software. Turn your photos into slides, add your affirmations as text, then set the presentation to the most inspiring music that you love! *Voilà*—your own vision movie for your business!

Key Category: Marketing and Sales

Selling a product or service may seem daunting, but developing a plan for your efforts while staying focused on the value of that product or service helps to make the process a pleasant experience. What is your plan for reaching your potential clients/customers and making them loyal and long-lasting champions of your business? Follow the same planning process provided in the Services and

Products section, for the analysis of this category utilizing the questions provided below:

1. Determine your 1-10 success rating.
2. Develop your key objectives.
3. Outline your strategies and action steps.

Questions to consider include:

Research

- What research have you conducted to understand your target market and their needs?
- Where do you find your target market?
- How well-served is your potential client base by competitors?

Foundation considerations

- Have you developed a logo and messaging that effectively reflect your business?
- Do you need/have business cards, stationery, or other promotional materials?
- Is an online presence important for your business? If so, have you developed one, and is it current and competitive?

Promotional activities

What promotional efforts and methods are you utilizing to make customers aware of your offerings and encouraging them to buy? How are they working for you?

- Professional/personal networking

- Referrals
- Events/tradeshows/workshops—participating and/or leading
- Virtual connections
- Technology usage
- Advertising
- Direct mail
- Sales
- How do you make the benefits and distinctions of your offerings clear to your audience?
- How do you re-inspire interest in your offerings to current clients?
- What systems do you have in place to close sales?

Inspirational Element: Quiet Time for Contemplation

We all understand the importance of finding time to listen to our hearts and inner guidance when it comes to our personal lives. Making the most of this time in our professional lives is equally as important. The best ideas—personal or professional—typically come in times of quiet consideration. Create this invaluable time as you plan and create your own professional masterpiece through one, or some, of the following methods:

- Meditation—Focused (on the breath, a chant, or music), Guided, or Moving
- Walking
- Prayer
- Journaling

Key Category: Finances

Last, but not least, it is imperative to consider the financial health of your business. Following the same process that you have for the other key business categories, consider the following questions and create your planning worksheets for this category.

Costs

- Have you calculated the annual and monthly costs of running your business?

- Are you consistently able to meet these costs through your business income?

- Do you include your salary in your monthly costs? If so, is this salary sufficient to meet your personal needs?

Cushion

- Do you have a rainy-day fund? If so, is this fund sufficient to cover at least six months of costs necessary to run your business?

Profit

- Are you seeing the fruits of your labors? Have you determined what level of profit would satisfy you? If so, are you meeting that objective?

Technology

- Are you utilizing a clear and effective system for tracking your finances and generating reports?

- If you have the technology to generate financial reports, do you use it by generating and reviewing income/cost summaries on at least a monthly basis?

People

- Do you have expert accounting support to assist you with questions and reporting activities?

Good Sense Business Elements

Take Action

I know people who just love the planning and researching process, but when it comes to implementing the wonderful ideas they have generated, the brakes slam on. Please, do not let this be you. Convert the major components of your plan onto your calendar or to-do list (or both), and make sure you take some kind of action on your plan every day.

Accountability

Studies have proven that people are exponentially more likely to accomplish their goals if they have discussed them with someone else. This creates a level of accountability that you are unable to achieve on your own, and who couldn't use outside support and another source of valuable ideas and possible opportunities?

Bump the sharing up a notch. Get an accountability partner to share ideas and commitments with on a daily basis or establish an accountability team of three people who meet weekly by phone to provide support to each other. First thing every morning, my accountability partner and I send each other an email listing our top five business development commitments for the day. We also report on how the prior day's tasks went. A second email may follow suggesting ideas or providing support. The entire daily process takes less than five minutes. Once each month, we schedule a telephone call to catch each other up on long-range goals and objectives. This past year has been my most successful ever in my business, and I attribute that success in large part to the accountability created through this partnership.

One more step up: Hire a coach—someone devoted to you and your success. This path will cost more, but the investment will be worth it.

Frequent Plan Review and Revision

Once you have your plan established, put on your calendar to review it at least once each week.

During each plan review, determine:

- Have the identified action steps been taken and in a timely manner?
- If no, why not?
- What "out-of-the-blue" opportunities arose?
- What roadblocks have been encountered in the implementation?
- How are stakeholders (you, clients, employees) reacting to the changes?
- What new inspirations have come to you?

To be most effective, your business plan, strategic plans, and the action steps resulting from them should adjust as the needs and priorities of your business change.

Cheers to your Inspired Planning and remember:

A goal without a plan is just a wish.

FRENCH AUTHOR AND POET, ANTOINE DE SAINT-EXUPERY

Connie's work, as owner of Scattered to Streamlined Business Coaching, is all about helping current and soon-to-be small business owners take those brilliant, but often scattered, business ideas and streamline them into plans, systems, and habits that create immediate and long-term success.

She is a business strategist and coach who helps her clients excel at their business endeavors by:

- Making business and strategic planning activities a top priority.

- Incorporating effective systems and work habits into day-to-day business activities.

- Providing motivation and accountability to create action in alignment with professional goals and planning objectives.

- Identifying and determining methods of overcoming challenges and areas of self-sabotage.

Having co-founded and run a management consulting firm for nineteen years and business coaching practice since 2011, Connie has worked with business owners, executives, and managers in a variety of fields and industries, including: business consulting, drug and alcohol testing, public transit, not-for-profit crisis care for children and group living support for adults, financial planning services, website design, information technology, and human resources. Regardless of the industry, core business development skills remain the same. It is Connie's passion to convey those skills and help others excel in their careers and business endeavors.

You may learn more about Connie and her work at: www.ScatteredtoStreamlined.com

CHAPTER 11

Leading a Heart-Centered Pivot and Reset in 3 Steps

by Lynden L. Kidd, JD

A worldwide pandemic, a national referendum on race, environmental disasters, and significant economic disruption and business failures—events in 2020 changed the world as we knew it. I am grateful I already had a personal experience that taught me the value of being heart-centered during times that required a pivot and reset. That's the message I wanted to share with my daughter and for our future generations of leaders to remember. So when what we knew to be normal transformed, I reflected on how we always continue to face change, and in November 2020, I wrote this letter to my then 18-year-old only child, Sophia:.

Dearest Daughter,

The world around us seems to be spinning like a top about to take off. I know you've noticed and felt the effects, too. But you and I are experienced at making necessary and prompt changes, aren't we? We have been on quite a roller coaster ride these last couple of years.

In the spring of your senior year of high school, everything screeched to a halt. Students were sent home, leaving behind cherished friendships built over the last four years or longer. Remote learning became the buzzword of the day. As we huddled with everyone else in the country, and for that fact the world, around our TVs and internet-fueled devices—hanging on every word of newscasters and special task forces—there was silence. Our world became surreal. Everything froze for a bit; then, we all began the pivot—the turn to something new. You and I have learned a lot about making quick changes. Many of these skills we acquired through significant adversity. It wasn't easy, but with each of our pivots, we learned to trust our hearts more and more.

Sophia, you've witnessed me survive. We left our normal behind in 2018 when I received the diagnosis of breast cancer. We learned the tough way to make better heart-centered decisions through our shared experience as we transformed. Like coal turning to diamond under heat and pressure, we grew stronger. Now we find ourselves, again, facing another opportunity to pivot. It was only recently that I came upon a social media post you had made about my discovering the lump, the subsequent diagnosis, the mastectomy, and the year of treatments. Your post sparked me to conclude that pivoting requires resilience and truth-telling. Good leaders everywhere have found ways to make the pivot seem elegant. Others have felt painfully clueless, frustrated, and even defeated in the turning point. Leadership isn't an "us" vs. "them" task. Each one of us, no matter our role in life or work, has a responsibility to show up as a leader and to be the best leader we can be for ourselves and others—no matter what crisis we face. That means listening to our hearts and finding a path forward that defies the fear of the moment.

You, my dearest, are an artist. You have been since you claimed that for yourself at age three. Now, you have a growing following on a social media site where you share your drawings and also offer to create commission works. As a young entrepreneur, leader, and influencer, your transparency is admirable and ever so needed in all of our leaders. Here is just one example that struck a chord in my heart:

"On a different note, you guys have probably noticed a decrease of art on my account. I won't go into too much detail, but my mom was diagnosed with cancer this past year, and it's been very hard on me and has left me very uninspired. I have full confidence that she'll make it out of this and be a survivor, but things like paying the medical bills are still going to take a toll, especially since it's just the two of us. I've been hiding this from pretty much everyone I'm not close to, but I figured it might be time to accept it. I hope you guys understand, and I'm grateful to all of you who have stuck around even though I haven't been very active. I'm wishing for a better year in 2019." (December 31, 2018)

That's a sobering post. I'm proud of you for sharing that with your followers. I wasn't aware you had become such an influencer. 2019 was crazier than in 2018. 2019 was a year of chemo and treatments. After the mastectomy, then surgical placement of a port to administer the drugs each week, my first cancer treatment was the week of Christmas 2018. Santa Momma wasn't very jolly that year. Treatments continued until the next year ending early December 2019. It was an arduous journey. I had that darn post-surgery drain attached to the fresh incision for what seemed like just short of forever. I lost my hair, shed plenty of tears, and succumbed to grumpy Mommy meltdowns. We ate many frozen dinners when I was so fatigued, I couldn't move another muscle to cook, and you had too much homework to help.

As I reflect, during this crazy time, I've seen how so much of what we learned remains relevant: We discovered how to make sense out of a world on tilt like a pinball machine. How to take the chaos of a scary uncharted, unscripted time and find a path through. In our situation, we faced the fear of the unknown, disbelief, financial uncertainty, and concern over if I would be able to work once treatments started. Then there was, what about you? Who would take care of you? My heart was heavy. Since your dad had died suddenly and unexpectedly when you were only seven, one of the first things you said to me after learning about my cancer was, "I don't want to be an orphan." That stung to my core. I remember saying, "I don't want that for you or me."

As our world learns to reset, I am grateful for what these lessons taught us. Here's how we pivoted, remember?

Step 1: Take 100% Responsibility

Especially in early 2019, you observed me through it all. That's the gift of families and marriages; we get to be close-up witnesses to one another's lives. That year, our world as we knew it blew up. Schedules changed. My energy flagged. There were many days when simply putting one foot in front of the other was the best I could do. You rallied. We faced our fears daily. We had no choice but to move through them—blood test results, doctors' appointments, and so much more. But we were lucky. I was fortunate. I had generous coworkers who helped me prepare the area around my port with numbing cream in the hours before weekly treatments, and others who let me leave meetings early or arrive late. We figured it out. We sorted. We pivoted. We brought our hearts to the challenge, and other co-conspirators in our success came with their hearts to support and rally us, too.

You might not realize this because I haven't said it enough, but you showed up beautifully. You demonstrated personal and professional leadership within our family, as a student, and with your own business. You listened to the call of your heart, and it emerged in your creativity. While you continued with your core themed drawings, you began exploring "lighter" subjects. You even offered a Bob Ross style "art class" for your friends. While you ached for me, you found a trail of good to follow. In your space, you led.

In 2020, the pandemic freeze extended into Spring Break, through your final taken-from-home AP exams, and your not-what-you-dreamed-of graduation. My heart again ached for you, for the fact that you would not experience the traditional, proud ceremony of your high school graduation, even though you'd been among the top 10 students of your class. You had dreamed of and worked toward being honored for that distinction on the graduation stage. I cried a lot about this when you and Grandma couldn't see.

As you know, over the last decade, I've learned transformational strategies and a coaching methodology, plus how better to evolve and grow my own business. I've had the privilege of learning, developing, and finding my voice in training with Jack Canfield, known as America's #1 Success Trainer and author of *The Success Principles*. In the spring of 2020, when I couldn't shake my tears and sorrow for you while deep in the quarantine, I wrote to Jack and asked for insight and inspiration. Never one to disappoint, he clarified the formula at the core of his #1 Success Principle. He responded to me with his heart, as he always modeled in his leadership.

$$\textbf{E (Event) + R (Response) = O (Outcome)}$$

Jack said:

This is a big issue of E+R=O. Our kids today are being faced with many problems and challenges we didn't face as kids—terrorism, environmental degradation and global warming, massive and rapid species extinction, major recessions, racial and social injustice, and economic disruptions, technology disruptions, social media distraction, and preoccupation with one's online image, and so much more. Now all of us have to step out of business as usual and step up to solve these problems.

As to E+R = O, it is not the E that is the biggest problem; it is our thinking that it shouldn't be so. Disappointment is making appointments with the future that the future doesn't keep, i.e. graduation, proms, etc.; the solution is to acknowledge what is (Byron Katie's The Work 101) and then be creative, i.e., create a different R—family graduation celebration, virtual Zoom call graduations and parties, [and only later] parties, and mock graduations in the future when it is OK to regather.

This is a time for all of us to WAKE UP to what isn't working in the world and not be caught in our idealized bubble.

Companies all around us in this pandemic pivot had to modify and change the way they did business. Honestly, I don't know a single company or person that escaped the need to change. Here's the deal: once I had a probable cancer diagnosis, I couldn't bury my head in the sand. I had to recognize that no matter what, the **O (Outcome)** depended on *me* to adjust (and that meant my life)! The same is expected—needed—in the business world. A pivot and reset require all leaders everywhere to reassess and readjust.

In the **E + R = O** formula, the only element that can be personally controlled is the **R (Response)**.

Sophia, let's examine this: what did—and what do—I still have responsibility for? The answer is always *my own* **Response**, which directly influences the outcome. If I choose to whine and fuss, then I have not taken responsibility and have acted as the victim by blaming someone or something else outside of me. If I chose to invite cancel-culture thinking by boycotting companies or disrespecting or unfollowing influencers because of something they do or say without taking the time to be curious and understand their why, I fall victim to my judgments, or even worse, unconscious bias. But, if I take 100% responsibility, then I know I am responsible for my role and my contribution to the outcome; and instead of playing victim, I step into a problem-solving and solution-focused mindset.

In 2018, getting to the problem-solving stage was tough. We went for a long time not knowing what was to happen next. We experienced weeks of not knowing the accurate diagnosis and the next steps. Much like in the 2020 and beyond pivot, we learned in waves. Ultimately, you and I didn't know until the post-

If I choose to whine and fuss, then I have not taken responsibility and have acted as the victim by blaming someone or something else outside of me. If I chose to invite cancel-culture thinking by boycotting companies or disrespecting or unfollowing influencers because of something they do or say without taking the time to be curious and understand their why, I fall victim to my judgments, or even worse, unconscious bias. But, if I take 100% responsibility, then I know I am responsible for my role and my contribution to the outcome; and instead of playing victim, I step into a problem-solving and solution-focused mindset.

mastectomy pathology report came back, that there were cancer cells, and they may have spread. We did our best. We made changes and adjustments that we thought made the most sense, not knowing if our treatment choices were the right ones. We were guided by doctors, scholarly articles, and conversations with those who had come before. We had to lean into choices and be guided by what seemed right in our hearts.

Just as we've seen recently with those in leadership, education, government, business, teams, or in volunteer situations, all are doing their best with pivots. No one had or has certainty. There's no Magic 8-Ball to guide us through the hardest decisions, but we all know a probable answer about our pivot choices: "Reply hazy, try again." We do not know what actions are going to bear fruit. However, we have been surprised—and relieved—by those actions that did.

So, dearest daughter, what do you have responsibility for? From my perspective, it is embracing what is—and allowing what has yet to come. I have responsibility for my response to the stresses of changes caused by the mayhem of this year, as do you. Our responses influence any outcome. If one chooses to see it, this year has also included remarkable innovation, new science, new policies, and new technology to help us both survive and thrive. You have responsibility for what you choose. What do you want to see?

Sophia, while I dearly tried to bury the fact that I found a lump and desperately wanted to wake up and have it gone, morning after morning for about two weeks—*Holy Hoover Dam!* it was still there. But I knew that this event (the lump) wasn't going to be managed unless I woke up from my disbelief and denial, stepped up, and moved on.

The heart-centered, awakened leader appreciates that any **Outcome** is dependent on their **Response** to the **Event**. No matter what the **Outcome** is, it results from the choices that the leader makes about the **Event**. As awakened leaders, we know we are not responsible for the **Events** of this time, but we are responsible for our role in **Responding** to them.

I'm proud of you, my dear Sophia, you decided to embrace **Event + Response = Outcome**. You took 100% responsibility by accepting what was happening to us, and in doing so, you also helped me. I am grateful.

Step 2: Communicate clearly about everything, all the time, and make decisions with heart

Daughter, as a model for others as well as a leader in school clubs and programs, you may have observed that the leader's role of strategic and tactical communication is crucial. Great leaders know being truthful, authentic, and transparent makes all the difference. Great leaders also know and appreciate that people who care are listening to what is said. In the case of our cancer story, the people who cared and had a stake in our conversations were employers, work colleagues, friends, and family. Suddenly, there was a spotlight on us (yes, they were worried about you, too). They wondered: What we would do, how we would react, what was going on with us, and how would we cope with my surgery and subsequent treatments?

Employees, team members, followers, vendors, and communities look to leaders for clues. Fear of the unknown can become paralyzing self-doubt for a leader. It takes courage to break free.

As days passed, with additional biopsies and awaiting the diagnosis, I was afraid, but I also didn't want to give in to the fear of the unknown and scare you *or me* too much. But I knew you needed to hear what was going on, constantly. For your wellbeing, I believed you needed to know when my next appointments would take place (milestones) and what was being measured (outcomes). I also know that I delivered some of those "messages" from my fear-filled heart. You chide me now because I seemed to be laughing and joking when I asked if you wanted to feel the lump in my breast (so you could know that it was real). Honestly, that was nervous laughter; I was frightened and trying to make an awkward discussion lighter-hearted.

In retrospect, I failed. That communication was flawed. You also chided me for first informing you about my lump when you were going out the door to school. You later told me you cried on the bus all the way. My timing may have been inelegant. Bad news can be tough to hear no matter when it is revealed, and I wanted to avoid being secretive. I'm sorry for my timing. Sometimes our timing is off, and when it is, we need to allow each other grace— especially in the heat and pressure of a pivot. My point is this: leaders of all walks (and scared Moms, too) need to be ready for tears. Resets aren't easy, yet giving ourselves and others grace to be heart-centered is necessary when choreographing a pivot— especially since news can't always be good and challenges can be grander than we ever fathomed.

We couldn't have pivoted without a team of supporters. Our care team members advocated for us and communicated information with family members, coworkers, and friends from near and far. On the day of surgery, Rachel, a close family friend, was armed with my phone to share updates with many who were anxious. Another best girlfriend, Debra, had flown in to stay with us for most of the first week post-surgery. She had all my personal items (as it was an outpatient surgery, and I was discharged later the same day). The messages shared by Rachel or Debra or you needed to be consistent, and each of you spoke for me when I couldn't speak for myself. Since Rachel went to almost every appointment and treatment with me, later during the chemo, I asked her from time to time to talk with you, to validate what was going on with my treatments. I wanted you to hear in another voice that I was progressing as expected—even if the news was tough.

With clients, customers, team members, vendors, and all other stakeholders, great leaders assure that communications are clear, detailed enough, and have heart, meaning they are empathetic with a call to action. In the pandemic pivot, companies splashed protocols across their websites concerning Covid-19 and included whether they were open; conducting part-time hours; or offering virtual services only. The key is they were communicating. They sent emails to their customers (we got so many) and posted messages on social media. Voicemail messages were changed, and signs were placed in windows. The rapid shifts required more attention to messaging. People needed to know how Covid-19 was affecting their services, staff, and customers. Consistent, relevant communication from more than one voice across multiple mediums was the hallmark.

The bottom line is that great leaders understand the need to talk about what is going on. If no communication is forthcoming, customers and others may assume:

- You've got it managed and don't need to talk about it (but they still wonder), or
- It isn't going well, and for some reason, you are embarrassed or reluctant to discuss it.

Essentially, it's vital to treat everyone as a valued stakeholder or shareholder, with equity in the outcome. In our cancer-related challenge, many counted: family, close friends, work colleagues, my boss, the boss's boss, the boss's boss's boss, your teachers, and the parents of your close friends. Eventually, it was your art customers too and my clients. For corporate leaders, it's clients, customers, vendors, shareholders, and stakeholders plus anyone in the supply chain or the distribution chain from potential new hires to the copy machine repair person.

Great heart-centered leaders know they need to invite all those people to make suggestions, to weigh-in on potential outcomes caused by hard times, look in the eyes of those scared others, and listen to their concerns and conclusions. In a pivot, we need to thoughtfully consider what's on their hearts too, and what is causing them concern—to meet them where they are in the moment, with grace. The heart-centered leader does not ignore the vested interest of others. For many, because they are an integral part of the processes, they may see something that we don't see; they may observe something that would be a solid resource that we don't know about or had not observed from our viewpoint.

For us, some of my girlfriends suggested that we conduct a GoFundMe campaign to help with medical expenses. At first, I resisted. I was painfully concerned and fearful that revealing what was going on with me, being so public, would show too much vulnerability. I was afraid of being that open. I was also consumed with worry about mounting medical bills. In retrospect, being vulnerable and authentic is never as painful as the worry. Letting go and allowing that GoFundMe Campaign to launch turned out to be financially lifesaving, and we received overwhelming support from all corners of our lives. It made a huge difference since we didn't have to fuss over finances and the large medical bills to pay when I was deep into my treatment.

Step 3: Chase the reflection of fear out of the decision as much as possible

When overwhelmed by fear of the unknown and the uncertainty of having to make decisions without a mirror to see around corners, it is tempting to just focus on the spreadsheet, numbers, and statistics for answers. That's a tough and difficult place for leaders to find themselves. The best leaders I've studied know to pause and to resist allowing others' fears to dictate their most intimate decisions, or to overly influence people-related cost-saving remedies such as how to deal with employee labor costs, reduction in pay, furloughs, layoffs, reduction in hiring, etc. They also consider how to manage independent contractors or others when making tough, tough decisions. They are champions for their people, listen, take counsel when needed, and most importantly, make decisions with heart.

During this year's pivots, many leaders were pained with difficult decisions to close businesses and displace employees. Yet when leaders made such decisions with heart and empathy, the people affected tended to pivot and bounce back faster. In aspects of my work, I've seen this first hand.

"It is a dangerous moment," said Fareed Zakariah, host of CNN's *Fareed Zakariah's GPS*, pointing to the warming planet, the increasing risk of pandemics and disasters like wildfires, slow economic growth, and looming tech disruptions. "But it is also in times like these that we can shape and alter such trends. ... People can choose which direction they want to push themselves, their societies, and their world."

In working with corporate leaders, displaced employees, and individuals who still have their jobs, yet feel overlooked or overwhelmed, I'm more grateful than ever for the work I do to help them pivot and transform.

Even you, Sophia, decided differently how you do your art. You pivoted from doing longer, bigger, more complex, and bigger commission projects to making some of your art available on a different platform and doing more whimsical stickers, which take less time. This shift in your life has allowed you to focus on different things such as college studies.

Conclusion—Pivot and pivot again: Ready, Fire, Aim & Adjust

There will always be a need to pivot to adapt to change. Leaders who pivot the best stay in front of the changes needed, perhaps just in front. They do this by making informed decisions but listening to their hearts. Then they make their pivots which allow the reset. They do their best to anticipate every possible scenario, and yet sometimes must confront the unexpected.

One last cancer treatment tale: starting late January, early February of 2019, a type of rash erupted. My skin had spots mostly on my arms and legs, and it was painful. The medical team didn't know exactly what to do except order more drugs to counteract it. When we first began treatment in December 2018, a large dose of steroids with the "chemo cocktail" was prescribed, which caused many uncomfortable side effects. We backed off of that dose slightly. But, when the rash started coming up, we discovered we had to go back to dosing with even more steroids. Honestly, the rash didn't go away. But it did become more manageable once the chemo part of the treatment regime ended. I still have residual effects from the rash almost two years later. However, I am blessed that we had available resources, and were able to do our best at the time with what we knew.

Heart-centered leaders do their best to stay out in front of needed pop-up changes while they continue to pivot. They anticipate that continuous course corrections are necessary to ensure the reset. The swiftest corrections require that we:

- Be *Ready*—We don't have more time.
- We *Fire*—We will never have a perfect solution, and staying in action is most important.
- We *Aim*—Keep targeting what we believe to be right.
- We, finally, *Adjust*, adjust, adjust, adjust.

Winston Churchill said,

"If you are going through hell, keep going."

We've been going through hell. And I have this to say—both to you, Sophia, and to other leaders who will read this:

Please keep going. Please honor your heart in the process and keep the interest of your people in sacred focus. Take responsibility for your reactions, face your fears, listen to your heart (over your fear of the unknown), and pivot and pivot and pivot; then reset and review. Agility, tenacity, and putting one foot in front of the other are the secrets to great heart-centered leadership. Together, we can create a visionary new reality. Great outcomes are a concerted effort.

Sophia, thanks for being on this journey with me. I am blessed to have your heart in our decisions and choices. We will continue to pivot and reset in our lives for many reasons. We will continue to cheer on awakened champions who lead with their hearts, helping us all to successfully pivot during these times of pandemic, racial bias, economic challenge, and environmental crisis—helping us to create our best reset, our best new normal.

With all my heart, I love you.

–Mom

A Canfield Methodologies Certified Trainer, Lynden Kidd, J.D. is a Talent Development Consultant, Career Strategist, and Executive Coach skilled in teaching the science of success. She has also been CEO of the healthcare and engineering recruiting firm, Next Iteration, for over a decade. Lynden has worked with hundreds of companies to identify, attract, retain, and develop key employees; to hire competitively, and to develop high performing teams. She also served as an Employability Coach supporting unemployed and underemployed people who were 50 years old or older to attract and find meaningful careers in the BACK TO WORK 50+ program locally in Tucson, AZ and now offering training for the National/Virtual BACK TO WORK 50+ program sponsored by the AARP Foundation.

Through a division of her company, Captivating Careers, Kidd has worked with leaders, managers, and highly skilled technical professionals. In their work with her, they became clearer about the role of work in their lives, became more effective corporate contributors, and have developed personalized career strategies designed to keep them on the path to fully engaged and satisfying work lives. Throughout Lynden's career, she has supported entrepreneurial ventures, as well as small business owners, to develop smart talent management skills so that they could retain more of their best people who were doing good while doing good for the company where they worked. Lynden's commitment is to lead others in transformations that soothe, empower, renew, restore, and replenish those who are career weary—especially professionals who are 40 years or beyond in their work lives. She hopes to inspire and guide thousands by offering heart-centered services about the nature of work and creativity, more specifically by creating communities where people can learn together. She offers live-supported digital courses, plus group and individual coaching options.

To learn more about Lynden, visit: https://linktr.ee/LyndenKidd

Epilogue

Your Invitation to Ignite Your Leadership and Share Your Greatness

*The most dangerous leadership myth is that leaders are born—that
there is a genetic factor to leadership. That's nonsense: in fact, the
opposite is true. Leaders are made rather than born.*

WARREN BENNIS, FOUNDING CHAIRMAN OF THE LEADERSHIP
INSTITUTE AT THE UNIVERSITY OF SOUTHERN CALIFORNIA

A lot has changed since *Ignite Your Leadership* was first
released a few years ago.

Today, it seems there is an increasing demand for strong
leaders to step up and inspire others to reconnect and share their
greatness with those they lead.

Globally, we're seeing a shift underway. Previous behaviors that
undermined individual authority of those we "managed" are no
longer being tolerated. We're being asked to consider the human
nature in our corporations and organizations. After all, organizations
are made up of people, and that must be remembered, particularly
in times of increasing challenges.

There are always things we can do to be part of this change.
We're all leaders—all of us. Our responsibility as leaders is to adapt
to change, while staying focused on our vision of new possibilities.
That takes honest awareness of ourselves, a willingness to try new
things, and being vulnerable in the process.

For instance, we can join in the conversation around hot topics such as leveraging technology, gender equality, racial bias, diversity, tolerance, transparency, and vulnerability. We can lean in and try new approaches to our challenges. We can model healthy behaviors such as self-care and boundary setting so that our "work" life doesn't overrun our "private" life, and thereby create a disconnect between who we are as leaders and who we are as loving, engaged friends and family members. This can be as simple as designating a technology-free day each week and setting off for a hike in the woods or a stroll in the park.

Essentially, to perform at our best consistently, self-care and overall wellness is critical. This means disconnecting from technology is a practice we have to adopt. Constantly "being on" does not give us the space to tap into our creativity or inner wisdom. Some of the greatest minds of all time frequently step (or stepped) away from their desks seeking inspiration and rejuvenation. Albert Einstein frequently took walks, and today, Brendon Burchard, Michael Hyatt, Oprah Winfrey, and Arianna Huffington remind us to unplug from our responsibilities. We have to take care of ourselves mentally, emotionally, and physically to encourage those we lead to do the same.

Our ability to lead is always being tested. Whenever there are problems in a team or an organization, strong leadership is key to finding solutions. Leading by example is a leader's responsibility. Those we lead are always watching what we do. They won't always do what we say, but they will follow our lead.

In *Ignite Your Leadership*, we covered how to lead ourselves, how to lead teams, and how to lead organizations as we deal with rapid change. Thank you for choosing to invest in your leadership.

We can always learn from other leaders and apply practices that help us become better leaders. The mastery of leadership is truly a journey that should never end.

We trust that this book will help ignite your leadership and support you in becoming the leader you can be—and perhaps the leader that you are being called to be. This is your invitation to step up and share your greatness with the world.

To your success,

Kathy Sparrow and Neel Raman, on behalf of our colleagues and coauthors

Need trainers or speakers?
Hire our authors!

Section 1: Leading Yourself

Kathy Sparrow ~ Chapter 1: The Power of Your Story: Discovering Your Why, Dissolving Your Why Nots. www.kathysparrow.com

Pete Winiarski ~ Chapter 2: Conscious Leadership: Leading Others by First Leading Yourself. www.petewiniarski.com

Nathalie Osborn ~ Chapter 3: Powering Personal Energy: The "kW" of Energized Leadership. www.nathalieosborn.com

Neel Raman ~ Chapter 4: Your Greatest Leadership Challenge Develop the Courage to LEAD www.neelraman.com

Sergio Sedas ~ Chapter 5: Intentional Possibility: The Magic of Happiness and the Power of Change. www.sergiosedas.com

Section 2: Leading Others

Sally Dooley ~ Chapter 6: Teams that Shine: Creating Conditions for Maximum Engagement. www.sallydooly.com

Jaroslav Průša ~ Chapter 7: Leadership at the Heart Level: Embracing and Implementing Change to Bring Meaningful Visions to Life. www.jaroslavprusa.cz

Jane Ransom ~ Chapter 8: How to Outfox the Three Subconscious Saboteurs Lurking in Your Workplace. www.janeransom.com

Section 3: Leading Organizations

Amina Makhdoom ~ Chapter 9: Leading Change: How to Create True, Meaningful, and Impactful Change in Your Organization. www.askamina.com and www.lunchwithcinderella.com

Connie Whitesell ~ Chapter 10: Planning with Passion: Business Strategizing for Inspired Leaders. www.ScatteredtoStreamlined.com

Lynden Kidd ~ Chapter 11: Leading a Heart-Centered Pivot and Reset in 3 Steps. www.lyndenkidd.com